Betty Crocker

the big book of Bisquick ®

Houghton Mifflin Harcourt

Boston • New York

GENERAL MILLS

Creative Content and Publishing Director: Elizabeth Nientimp

Food Content Marketing Manager: Heather Reid Liebo

Senior Editor: Grace Wells

Food Editor: Catherine Swanson

Recipe Development and Testing: Betty Crocker Kitchens

Photography: General Mills Photography Studios and Image Library

HOUGHTON MIFFLIN HARCOURT

Publisher: Natalie Chapman

Editorial Director: Cindy Kitchel

Executive Editor: Anne Ficklen

Editorial Associate: Molly Aronica

Managing Editor: Marina Padakis

Associate Production Editor: Helen Seachrist

Cover Design: Tai Blanche

Interior Design and Layout: Tai Blanche

Senior Production Coordinator: Kimberly Kiefer

www.hmhco.com

Library of Congress Cataloging-in-Publication Data is available.

ISBN 978-0-544-61654-7 (paperback); 978-0-544-67193-5 (ebk)

Manufactured in the United States of America

DOC 10 9 8 7 6 5 4 3 2   4500568249

Cover photos: Shrimp and Artichoke Quiche (page 250), Double-Berry Doughnuts (page 70), Impossibly Easy Mexican Mini Veggie Pies (page 216), Impossibly Easy Raspberry–Cream Cheese Muffins (page 92), Cheesecake Pancakes (page 154), Gluten-Free Ultimate Chicken Fingers (page 56)

The Betty Crocker Kitchens seal guarantees success in your kitchen. Every recipe has been tested in America's Most Trusted Kitchens™ to meet our high standards of reliability, easy preparation and great taste.

FIND MORE GREAT IDEAS AT
BettyCrocker.com

Dear Friends,

Since 1930, Bisquick has been there for all of us as an easy way to make tasty homemade biscuits, tender pancakes, fabulous desserts and even hearty main dishes. Times have changed, but be assured that Bisquick is still the same wonderful baking mix that you remember. Changes have come with new products in the lineup including offerings of Gluten-Free Bisquick, Heart-Smart Bisquick and even a new pancake mix.

In *The Big Book of Bisquick*, you'll find recipes for every occasion, all using one of the unique Bisquick products. There's variety in every chapter, from warm appetizers and creative breads to new ideas for pancakes or pizza and even an array of desserts and treats to choose from. Why not bake up a tasty savory pie for dinner? Impossibly Easy Beef, Broccoli and Mushroom Pie on page 240 is one of our test kitchen favorites and it's so easy to make. Or, for a wonderful breakfast treat, how about yummy baked Double-Berry Doughnuts on page 70—they're sure to bring rave reviews from family and friends.

Also, for those times when you want to have fun and create, check out the "Make It Your Way" feature on page 230. You will see that it's easy to mix and match ingredients of your choice to design your own Impossibly Easy Pie. There are also fun ideas for topping sugar cookies and biscuits that you'll want to try.

So it's your choice which product to use, but you can be sure that the recipe chosen will be easy to make and delicious because it starts with Bisquick!

Happy Cooking,
Betty Crocker

Look for these helpful icons:

Quick

30 minutes or less

Calorie Controlled

Complete/One-Dish Meal:
550 calories or less

Main Dish/Plain Meat/Main Dish Salad/Soups/Stews/Chilies:
400 calories or less

Side Dish/Side Dish Salad/ Snack/Bread/Appetizer:
200 calories or less

Desserts:
200 calories or less

contents

BISQUICK—THE HISTORY IS IN THE MIX

In 1930, Carl Smith, a General Mills sales executive, was travelling by train between Portland, Oregon, and San Francisco. While dining aboard the train, though it was well past mealtime, Smith was served a plate of delicious, hot, homemade biscuits. He was amazed and curious how the cook could produce hot biscuits so quickly. What was the chef's secret? He had blended flour with fat, baking powder and salt in advance and stored the mixture in an ice chest. Starting with this mix, he could quickly make biscuits-to-order in just a few minutes.

This was an entirely new idea. Smith recognized the potential that a premixed baking mix could have for home bakers, and took the idea to Charlie Kress, the chief chemist at General Mills. The challenges of trying to create the proper proportions of ingredients into a mix that could make biscuits as good as or better than homemade were significant. The resulting efforts became Bisquick mix.

1930s
Bisquick Beginnings

- Less than a year after the dining car discovery, Bisquick was on the market—and an immediate success!

- Competitors quickly jumped on the baking mix bandwagon. Within a year, 95 other biscuit mixes were introduced.

- Only six competitors survived the following year . . . all trailing behind sales of Bisquick.

1940s
Bisquick Makes It Easy

- With America at war, families came to depend on the convenience of Bisquick.

- The Betty Crocker Kitchens developed great-tasting recipes using Bisquick for every meal occasion, giving Bisquick the slogan, "A world of baking in a box."

1950s
Bisquick: One Good Mix

- In the '50s, the ad slogan "12 Good Things from One Good Mix!" was introduced, showing how Bisquick easily made biscuits, shortcake, pancakes and more.

- The most popular recipes started appearing on the familiar yellow box, and many are still printed on Bisquick packages today.

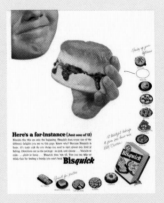

1960s
New Bisquick Enters the Scene

- New Bisquick was introduced, designed to appeal to makers of southern-style biscuits—"Makes biscuits lighter and fluffier than scratch!"

- The reformulated Bisquick performed so well in test markets that it was rolled out into national distribution to replace regular Bisquick and "New" was dropped from the name.

1970s
Bisquick Cookbook: A Huge Success

- Packed with more than 200 recipes for breads, main dishes and desserts, a cookbook was introduced to help promote Bisquick as a multipurpose mix.

- The cookbook was a raging success and by 1979 was in its 8th printing.

1980s
Milestones in Bisquick History

- Hundreds of thousands of Bisquick fans joined the Bisquick Recipe Club, receiving the "Bisquick Banner," a quarterly newsletter that featured relevant articles and recipes for family meals as well as entertaining ideas.

- Impossible Coconut Pie was created. It was known as "the pie that does the impossible—and forms its own crust."

- Soon more than 100 sweet or savory Impossible Pie recipes were created in the Betty Crocker Kitchens.

- Renamed Impossibly Easy Pies, these recipes continue to be requested favorites, as they still meet the needs of families for fast and easy meal and dessert solutions.

1990s
Bisquick Still Relevant to Cooks

- A desire to return to simplicity and use trusted favorites helped Bisquick remain a staple in homes across America.

- People were drawn to the comfort of fresh-baked breads, pizzas and one-dish meals. Bisquick provided the way to easily make these dishes—even with schedules that became busier than ever.

2000s
And Beyond: Bisquick Your Way

- Today, Bisquick remains a household word and the country's premiere convenience baking mix, more than eighty years after its introduction.

- Bisquick meets the dietary needs of families with Original, Heart Smart and Gluten Free varieties that are now available.

FAQ About Bisquick and Baking

Start with Bisquick, and you can have a wide variety of easy, quick homemade dishes in no time! It's a fantastic must-have for your pantry. If you've got questions about baking with Bisquick, look here for answers to the most frequently asked questions.

Bisquick Basics

Q: What's the best way to measure Bisquick?

A: Spoon Bisquick into a dry-ingredient measuring cup (no sifting required), and level with a straight-edged knife or spatula—don't pack it in or tap the cup, to avoid over-measuring.

Q: Can I use Bisquick in recipes calling for flour?

A: Bisquick contains fat and leavening as well as flour, so you can't use it as a straight substitute for flour in baked goods, such as cookies or cakes. However Bisquick can be directly substituted for flour to thicken a stew or gravy.

Q: How should I store Bisquick?

A: Keep it fresh by storing it in an airtight container or plastic bag in a cool, dry place, such as your pantry shelf. If you wish to store it for a long period of time, keep it in the refrigerator or freezer. (If frozen, just bring to room temperature before using.)

Q: Will Bisquick be affected by humidity?

A: Bisquick will react to the environment just like any other flour-based product does. In humid conditions, you may find that dough and batters are stickier, softer or more fluid. You can add small additional amounts of Bisquick to make the dough or batter easier to work with.

Q: Can I substitute Bisquick Heart Smart® or Bisquick® Gluten Free mixes in recipes calling for Original Bisquick® mix?

A: Bisquick Heart Smart® was designed for those who need to watch their fat and cholesterol intake. Bisquick Gluten Free® was designed to give those with gluten sensitivities the recipes they crave, without the gluten. Because the formulas are different, the products may not perform successfully in other recipes.

Also, simply substituting Bisquick Heart Smart® for Original Bisquick® does not ensure that the recipe is appropriate for someone needing a lower-fat/cholesterol recipe. Other ingredients in the recipes may be higher in fat and cholesterol and therefore not appropriate for someone watching their fat and cholesterol intake. Likewise, substituting Bisquick Gluten Free® for Original Bisquick® may not ensure that a recipe is gluten-free. They may contain gluten—without you realizing it—which would not be appropriate for anyone needing gluten-free recipes.

Bisquick Pancakes and Waffles

Q: Why are my pancakes or waffles raw in the center?

A: Too little liquid or too much Bisquick could cause the thicker batter not to cook through the center. Or the griddle temperature may be too high.

Q: Can Bisquick pancake batter be prepared ahead of time?

A: You could make the batter, then cover and refrigerate it up to 1 hour ahead. Any longer than that could deactivate the leavening, causing the pancakes to be flat rather than fluffy, and the batter will become too thick.

Q: Why are my pancakes or waffles leathery and tough?

A: If the griddle temperature is too low, it takes longer for the pancakes to brown, so they can become dry and tough. If the griddle is too hot, the pancake edges can get overcooked quickly and become tough.

Q: Can I use buttermilk in pancakes or waffles?

A: Yes—just use the same amount of buttermilk as milk or water called for in the recipe.

Q: What's the best way to store leftover pancakes and waffles?

A: Cool pancakes or waffles completely on a cooling rack. Store them in an airtight container or resealable food-storage plastic bag in the refrigerator no longer than 2 days or in the freezer for up to 3 months. Microwave one frozen pancake or waffle uncovered on a microwavable plate on High 20 to 30 seconds or three pancakes at a time, about 1 minute. Or, pop a pancake or waffle in the toaster to reheat.

Q: Why are my waffles crispy?

A: You may have over-sprayed or -greased your waffle iron, or you may have used too much liquid and not enough Bisquick mix.

Bisquick Muffins

Q: Why are my muffins peaked and full of holes?

A: You may have overmixed the batter, or your oven temperature is too high.

Q: Why didn't my muffins rise?

A: You may have undermixed the batter, or your oven temperature is too low.

Q: Why are my muffins tough, heavy and rubbery?

A: You may have overmixed the batter, or you used too much egg—large eggs were used when developing the recipes, so using extra-large eggs could cause this.

Bisquick Biscuits

Q: Why didn't my biscuits rise?

A: Too much liquid, too little Bisquick, or too little or too gently mixing/kneading.

Q: Why are my biscuits tough and hard?

A: Overmixing or over-kneading, oven temperature too high or bake time too long, over-measurement of Bisquick or too little liquid.

Q: Why is my biscuit dough sticky?

A: Under-measurement of Bisquick, over-measurement of liquid or humid conditions, causing the Bisquick to be stickier than usual.

Bisquick Shortcakes

Q: Why are my shortcakes raw or doughy in the center?

A: Under-measurement of liquid or over-measurement of Bisquick (see the Q&A for measuring Bisquick, page 8) are two common reasons. Oven temperature might be too high. Do not underbake shortcake.

Q: Why is the bottom crust of my shortcake dark?

A: Shortcakes tend to have dark bottom crusts, due to their sugar content. Choose shiny metal pans (not dark pans) for more even browning—top and bottom. If your pans are dark (or darkened from an accumulation of fat when baking), try reducing the oven temperature to 400°F. Bake shortcakes on a cookie sheet in the center of the oven.

Q: Why do my shortcakes stick to the cookie sheet?

A: It's typical for drop shortcakes to stick slightly to the cookie sheet. Be sure to remove them from the cookie sheet immediately after baking, using a metal spatula or pancake turner. A clean cookie sheet is essential—make sure to remove all grease, crumbs or baked-on dough before using for the best results.

CHAPTER 1

Anytime Snacks & Appetizers

Gluten-Free Mushroom-Pecan Appetizers

Prep Time: 15 Minutes • **Start to Finish:** 1 Hour 15 Minutes • **24 appetizers**

2 tablespoons butter

1 package (8 oz) sliced fresh mushrooms (about 3 cups)

1 cup chopped onions (2 medium)

2 cups shredded Swiss cheese (8 oz)

1 cup chopped pecans, toasted*

1 box (9 oz) frozen chopped spinach, thawed, squeezed to drain**

3 eggs

1⅓ cups milk

¾ cup Bisquick® Gluten Free mix

1 teaspoon salt

1 teaspoon garlic powder

1 Heat oven to 400°F. Spray 13x9-inch pan with cooking spray (without flour).

2 In 10-inch skillet, melt butter over medium heat. Add mushrooms and onions; cook about 5 minutes, stirring occasionally, until onion is tender. Drain.

3 In pan, mix mushroom mixture, cheese, pecans and spinach; spread evenly. In medium bowl, stir all remaining ingredients with whisk or fork until blended. Pour evenly into pan.

4 Bake 25 to 30 minutes or until knife inserted in center comes out clean. Cool 30 minutes before serving.

*To toast pecans, cook in an ungreased skillet over medium heat 5 to 7 minutes, stirring frequently, until golden brown.

**To quickly thaw spinach, cut a small slit in the center of the pouch; microwave on High 2 to 3 minutes or until thawed. Remove spinach from the pouch; squeeze dry with paper towels.

1 Appetizer: Calories 120; Total Fat 8g (Saturated Fat 3g; Trans Fat 0g); Cholesterol 40mg; Sodium 180mg; Total Carbohydrate 6g (Dietary Fiber 1g); Protein 5g **Exchanges:** ½ Low-Fat Milk, ½ Vegetable, 1 Fat **Carbohydrate Choices:** ½

> If you are cooking gluten free, always read labels to make sure each recipe ingredient is gluten free. Products and ingredient sources can change.

Tomato-Artichoke Appetizers

Prep Time: 45 Minutes • **Start to Finish:** 1 Hour • 30 appetizers

2 cups Original Bisquick® mix

½ cup boiling water

¾ cup mayonnaise

¾ cup grated Parmesan cheese

½ teaspoon onion juice, if desired

1 jar (7.5 oz) marinated artichokes, chopped

30 thin slices plum (Roma) tomatoes (4 to 5 medium)

Parsley sprigs

1 Heat oven to 400°F. Grease large cookie sheet or spray with cooking spray.

2 In medium bowl, stir Bisquick mix and boiling water; beat vigorously 20 strokes. Place dough on surface sprinkled with Bisquick mix; gently roll in Bisquick mix to coat. Knead 10 times.

3 Roll dough to ⅛-inch thickness. With 2-inch round cutter dipped in Bisquick mix, cut dough into 30 rounds. Place about 2 inches apart on cookie sheet.

4 In small bowl, mix mayonnaise, cheese and onion juice; mix well. Spread ½ teaspoon mayonnaise mixture on each dough round. Top with scant 1 teaspoon artichokes and ½ teaspoon mayonnaise mixture. Place 1 slice tomato on each round; top with 1 teaspoon mayonnaise mixture.

5 Bake 10 to 12 minutes or until golden brown and puffy. Garnish with parsley. Serve warm or at room temperature.

1 Appetizer: Calories 90; Total Fat 7g (Saturated Fat 1.5g; Trans Fat 0g); Cholesterol 0mg; Sodium 190mg; Total Carbohydrate 7g (Dietary Fiber 1g); Protein 2g **Exchanges:** ½ Starch, 1½ Fat **Carbohydrate Choices:** ½

Tomato-Artichoke Appetizers is a 2013 Bisquick Family Favorites Recipe Contest award-winning recipe developed by Karen Haldeman, 2nd Place, Ohio State Fair (Columbus, OH).

Mini Pancake-Avocado Stacks

Prep Time: 1 Hour 20 Minutes • **Start to Finish:** 1 Hour 20 Minutes • 18 servings

1 cup Original Bisquick® mix

½ cup milk

2 tablespoons real maple syrup or maple-flavored syrup

1 egg

½ cup chopped cooked bacon (about 8 slices)

¼ cup shredded Cheddar cheese (1 oz)

2 tablespoons chopped green onions

2 ripe medium avocados, pitted, peeled

1 teaspoon fresh lemon juice

⅛ teaspoon ground red pepper (cayenne)

⅛ teaspoon salt

9 red or yellow cherry tomatoes, cut in half

18 fancy toothpicks

1 In medium bowl, stir Bisquick mix, milk, syrup and egg with whisk or fork until blended. In small bowl, reserve 2 tablespoons cooked bacon. Stir remaining bacon, the cheese and green onions into batter.

2 Heat nonstick griddle or 12-inch nonstick skillet over medium-low heat (350°F). Brush griddle with vegetable oil if necessary.

3 For each pancake, spoon 1 teaspoon batter onto hot griddle, making 54 silver dollar–size pancakes. Cook until edges are dry. Turn; cook other side until golden brown.

4 In medium bowl, mash avocado, lemon juice, red pepper and salt with fork until blended (mixture will be lumpy).

5 For each pancake stack, spoon 1 teaspoon avocado mixture onto center of 3 pancakes. Stack pancakes, pressing down lightly to spread avocado mixture to edges. Repeat with remaining pancakes and avocado mixture. Top each stack with small amount reserved bacon and a tomato half; secure with toothpick. Serve immediately, or refrigerate up to 3 hours. If refrigerated, let stand at room temperature 15 minutes before serving.

1 Serving: Calories 90; Total Fat 5g (Saturated Fat 1.5g; Trans Fat 0g); Cholesterol 15mg; Sodium 170mg; Total Carbohydrate 8g (Dietary Fiber 1g); Protein 2g **Exchanges:** ½ Starch, 1 Fat **Carbohydrate Choices:** ½

> Look for ripe avocados that yield to gentle pressure but are still just slightly firm. If you can only find firm avocados, just let them stand at room temperature for a day or two until they ripen.

Mini Corn Cakes

Prep Time: 25 Minutes • **Start to Finish:** 25 Minutes • 24 servings (1 corn cake and 1 teaspoon sour cream each)

1 tablespoon butter

⅓ cup chopped green onions (about 5 medium)

⅓ cup chopped celery

⅓ cup chopped red bell pepper

1 cup soft white bread crumbs (about 1½ slices bread)

½ cup Original Bisquick® mix

1 teaspoon sugar

½ teaspoon salt

⅛ teaspoon ground red pepper (cayenne)

2 eggs, slightly beaten

1 can (11 oz) whole kernel sweet corn, drained

2 tablespoons vegetable oil

½ cup chive-and-onion sour cream potato topper (from 12-oz container)

1 In 12-inch nonstick skillet, melt butter over medium heat. Add onions, celery and bell pepper; cook 3 minutes, stirring occasionally.

2 In medium bowl, stir onion mixture, bread crumbs, Bisquick mix, sugar, salt, red pepper, eggs and corn until well blended.

3 In same skillet, heat 2 teaspoons of the oil over medium heat. Drop 8 tablespoonfuls of corn mixture into oil, spreading each to 1½-inch round. Cook 2 to 3 minutes, carefully turning once, until golden brown. Cook remaining corn cakes in 2 batches of 8 each, using 2 teaspoons oil for each batch. Serve with sour cream topper.

1 Serving: Calories 60; Total Fat 3.5g (Saturated Fat 1.5g; Trans Fat 0g); Cholesterol 20mg; Sodium 135mg; Total Carbohydrate 5g (Dietary Fiber 0g); Protein 1g **Exchanges:** ½ Starch, ½ Fat **Carbohydrate Choices:** ½

Sriracha Veggie-Cheese Balls and Sauce

Prep Time: 25 Minutes • **Start to Finish:** 50 Minutes • 25 servings (1 ball and about 1 teaspoon sauce each)

VEGGIE-CHEESE BALLS

- 2 cups frozen chopped broccoli, thawed, squeezed to drain
- 2 cups shredded Colby–Monterey Jack cheese blend (8 oz)
- 1 cup Original Bisquick® mix
- 1 egg
- 1 tablespoon finely chopped red bell pepper
- 1 teaspoon garlic salt
- 1 to 2 teaspoons Sriracha sauce

SAUCE

- ½ cup sour cream
- 2 teaspoons Sriracha sauce
- 2 tablespoons sliced green onions (2 medium)
- 2 tablespoons finely chopped red bell pepper

1 Heat oven to 350°F. Grease bottom and sides of 15x10x1-inch pan with shortening or cooking spray.

2 In large bowl, stir veggie-cheese ball ingredients until blended. With wet hands, shape mixture into 25 (1-inch) balls; place in pan.

3 Bake 20 to 25 minutes or until golden brown.

4 Meanwhile, in small bowl, mix sauce ingredients. Immediately remove cheese balls from pan. Serve warm with sauce for dipping.

1 Serving: Calories 70; Total Fat 4.5g (Saturated Fat 2.5g; Trans Fat 0g); Cholesterol 20mg; Sodium 170mg; Total Carbohydrate 4g (Dietary Fiber 0g); Protein 3g **Exchanges:** ½ Starch, 1 Fat **Carbohydrate Choices:** 0

These cheese balls are easy to make ahead. Choose from these methods:

Cover and refrigerate unbaked veggie-cheese balls up to 24 hours. Bake as directed.

Cover and freeze unbaked veggie-cheese balls up to 1 month. Heat oven to 350°F. Place frozen veggie-cheese balls on ungreased cookie sheet. Bake 25 to 30 minutes or until brown.

Bake as directed; cover and freeze up to 1 month. Heat oven to 350°F. Place frozen veggie-cheese balls on ungreased cookie sheet. Bake 10 to 12 minutes or until heated through.

Bake as directed; cover and freeze up to 1 month. Place 6 frozen veggie-cheese balls on microwavable plate. Loosely cover with waxed paper. Microwave on High 45 seconds to 1 minute or until heated through.

Apple-Cheese Balls

Prep Time: 1 Hour 10 Minutes • **Start to Finish:** 1 Hour 30 Minutes • 48 appetizers

1¾ cups Bisquick Heart Smart® mix

½ cup applesauce

½ cup finely chopped peeled apple

¼ cup milk

2 teaspoons chopped fresh parsley

2 cups shredded reduced-fat Cheddar cheese (8 oz)

1 Heat oven to 350°F. Lightly spray 15x10x1-inch pan with cooking spray.

2 In large bowl, stir all ingredients until well blended, using hands if necessary.

3 Onto pan, drop mixture by rounded teaspoonfuls about 1½ inches apart.

4 Bake 16 to 18 minutes or until golden brown. Immediately remove from pan. Serve warm.

1 Appetizer: Calories 25; Total Fat 0.5g (Saturated Fat 0g; Trans Fat 0g); Cholesterol 0mg; Sodium 95mg; Total Carbohydrate 4g (Dietary Fiber 0g); Protein 2g **Exchanges:** ½ Other Carbohydrate **Carbohydrate Choices:** 0

Use a small scoop, about 1⅛ inches in diameter, to make spooning and dropping the mixture faster and easier.

Spinach-Cheese Balls

Prep Time: 10 Minutes • **Start to Finish:** 25 Minutes • **30 appetizers**

1 box (9 oz) frozen chopped spinach, thawed, squeezed to drain*

1 cup Original Bisquick® mix

2 cups shredded mozzarella cheese (8 oz)

1 egg

2 teaspoons Italian seasoning

1 teaspoon garlic salt

1 cup tomato pasta sauce, heated, if desired

1 Heat oven to 400°F. Spray cookie sheet with cooking spray.

2 In large bowl, mix all ingredients except pasta sauce until blended. Shape mixture into 30 (1-inch) balls; place on cookie sheet about 1 inch apart.

3 Bake 10 to 15 minutes or until golden brown. Immediately remove from pan. Serve with pasta sauce.

*To quickly thaw spinach, cut small slit in center of pouch; microwave on High 2 to 3 minutes or until thawed. Remove spinach from pouch; squeeze dry with paper towels.

1 Appetizer: Calories 45; Total Fat 2g (Saturated Fat 1g; Trans Fat 0g); Cholesterol 10mg; Sodium 130mg; Total Carbohydrate 3g (Dietary Fiber 0g); Protein 3g **Exchanges:** ½ High-Fat Meat **Carbohydrate Choices:** 0

Red Pepper–Filled Appetizer Hearts

Prep Time: 15 Minutes • **Start to Finish:** 50 Minutes • 24 appetizers

1½ cups Original Bisquick® Mix

2 teaspoons dried oregano leaves

⅓ cup water

¼ cup garlic-and-herbs spreadable cheese (from 6.5-oz container)

½ cup finely chopped red bell pepper

2 tablespoons butter, melted

1 In medium bowl, stir Bisquick mix, oregano and water until stiff dough forms. Place dough on surface sprinkled with Bisquick mix; gently roll in Bisquick mix to coat. Knead 5 times. Roll dough into 13x10-inch rectangle, about ⅛ inch thick.

2 In small bowl, mix cheese and bell pepper. Spread mixture evenly over dough. Carefully roll long edges of dough to meet in center. Place on cookie sheet lined with cooking parchment paper. Freeze 10 to 15 minutes or until firm.

3 Meanwhile, heat oven to 400°F. Spray large cookie sheet with cooking spray.

4 Transfer dough to cutting board. With sharp knife, cut dough into 24 (½-inch) slices. Place slices, cut side down, on sprayed cookie sheet. Slightly pinch base of heart into point. Brush butter over hearts.

5 Bake 7 to 9 minutes or until tops are light golden brown. Cool 10 minutes before serving.

1 Appetizer: Calories 45; Total Fat 2g (Saturated Fat 1g; Trans Fat 0g); Cholesterol 0mg; Sodium 95mg; Total Carbohydrate 5g (Dietary Fiber 0g); Protein 0g **Exchanges:** ½ Other Carbohydrate, ½ Fat **Carbohydrate Choices:** ½

These heart-shaped appetizers are the perfect starter to a romantic Valentine's Day dinner.

Serve these flavorful little biscuits alongside a Greek salad.

Cheesy Broccoli Puffs with Sriracha Mayonnaise

Prep Time: 20 Minutes • **Start to Finish:** 1 Hour • 12 servings (2 puffs and 2 teaspoons mayonnaise each)

PUFFS

- 1 bag (12 oz) frozen broccoli & cheese sauce
- ¾ cup Original Bisquick® mix
- ½ teaspoon crushed red pepper flakes
- ⅛ teaspoon salt
- ½ cup milk
- 2 eggs
- ⅓ cup grated Parmesan cheese
- 6 slices packaged precooked bacon, chopped

MAYONNAISE

- ½ cup mayonnaise
- 2 teaspoons Sriracha sauce
- Sliced green onions, if desired

1 Heat oven to 375°F. Generously grease 24 mini muffin cups with shortening or cooking spray. Cook broccoli as directed on bag for minimum time. Chop broccoli.

2 In medium bowl, stir Bisquick mix, crushed red pepper, salt, milk and eggs with whisk or fork until blended. Stir in broccoli and cheese sauce, Parmesan cheese and bacon. Divide mixture evenly among muffin cups (cups will be full).

3 Bake 16 to 18 minutes or until toothpick inserted in center comes out clean and tops are light brown. Cool 5 minutes. With thin knife, loosen sides of puffs from pan; remove to cooling rack.

4 Meanwhile, in small bowl, mix mayonnaise and Sriracha sauce until smooth. Top each warm puff with about 1 teaspoon mayonnaise mixture; garnish with green onions.

1 Serving: Calories 120; Total Fat 7g (Saturated Fat 2g; Trans Fat 0g); Cholesterol 40mg; Sodium 460mg; Total Carbohydrate 9g (Dietary Fiber 0g); Protein 5g **Exchanges:** ½ Starch, ½ Medium-Fat Meat, 1 Fat **Carbohydrate Choices:** ½

For vegetarian guests, substitute ¼ cup finely chopped red or green bell pepper or 2 tablespoons sliced green onions for the bacon.

If you just have one 12-cup mini muffin pan, refrigerate the remaining batter while baking the first puffs. Wash and grease the pan before filling with additional batter. The baking time may be a minute or two longer if the batter is cold.

Rosemary-Madeira Baked Brie

Prep Time: 15 Minutes • **Start to Finish:** 1 Hour 15 Minutes • **8 servings**

2	teaspoons olive oil
1	cup Original Bisquick® mix
4½	teaspoons chopped fresh rosemary leaves
¼	cup Madeira wine
2	tablespoons half-and-half
1	round (8 oz) Brie cheese
¼	cup apricot preserves

1 Heat oven to 350°F. Line cookie sheet with cooking parchment paper. Spoon 1 teaspoon of the oil in center of parchment paper; spread to 5-inch round.

2 In medium bowl, mix Bisquick mix and rosemary. In small bowl, mix wine and half-and-half. Stir wine mixture into Bisquick mixture; beat vigorously 20 strokes.

3 Place dough on surface generously sprinkled with Bisquick mix; gently roll in Bisquick mix to coat. Knead 10 times. Divide dough in half; shape each half into a ball.

4 Place 1 ball on parchment paper in center of oil; press and shape into 5-inch round. Place cheese on center of dough. Press and shape second ball into 6-inch round; place dough over cheese. Pinch edges of dough to seal. Brush top and sides with remaining 1 teaspoon oil.

5 Bake 25 to 30 minutes or until light golden brown. Cool 30 minutes. Serve with preserves.

1 Serving: Calories 210; Total Fat 12g (Saturated Fat 6g; Trans Fat 0.5g); Cholesterol 30mg; Sodium 360mg; Total Carbohydrate 18g (Dietary Fiber 0g); Protein 7g **Exchanges:** 1 Starch, ½ Low-Fat Milk, 2 Fat **Carbohydrate Choices:** 1

Rosemary-Madeira Baked Brie is a 2013 Bisquick Family Favorites Recipe Contest award-winning recipe developed by Susan Christen of Oceanside, 2nd Place, San Diego County Fair (CA).

Feta Cheese Squares

Prep Time: 10 Minutes • **Start to Finish:** 50 Minutes • **60 appetizers**

2 cups Original Bisquick® mix

1½ teaspoons baking powder

¼ teaspoon salt

1 cup milk

½ cup butter, melted

4 packages (4 oz each) crumbled herb-and-garlic feta cheese (4 cups)

1 container (8 oz) small-curd cottage cheese

3 eggs, slightly beaten

1 Heat oven to 350°F. Lightly spray 15x10x1-inch pan with cooking spray.

2 In large bowl, mix Bisquick mix, baking powder and salt. Add remaining ingredients, stirring just until moistened. Spoon into pan; spread evenly.

3 Bake 30 minutes or until golden brown and set. Cool in pan on cooling rack 10 minutes. Cut into 10 rows by 6 rows; serve warm.

1 Appetizer: Calories 59; Total Fat 4g (Saturated Fat 2g; Trans Fat 0g); Cholesterol 0mg; Sodium 191mg; Total Carbohydrate 4g (Dietary Fiber 0g); Protein 3g **Exchanges:** ½ Medium-Fat Meat, ½ Fat **Carbohydrate Choices:** 0

Gluten-Free Chipotle Cheese Crackers

Prep Time: 15 Minutes • **Start to Finish:** 45 Minutes • 24 crackers

¼ cup butter, softened

1 cup Bisquick® Gluten Free mix

2 cups shredded gluten-free sharp Cheddar cheese

1 teaspoon gluten-free Worcestershire sauce

½ teaspoon chipotle chili powder

½ teaspoon salt

1 egg

1 Heat oven to 400°F. Line cookie sheet with cooking parchment paper.

2 In large bowl, mix all ingredients with spoon or hands until thoroughly blended. Form dough into 24 (1½-inch) balls. Place about 2 inches apart on cookie sheet. Flatten balls to 2½-inch diameter with fingers or bottom of drinking glass.

3 Bake 14 to 16 minutes or until edges are beginning to brown. Remove from cookie sheet; cool on cooling rack.

1 Cracker: Calories 80; Total Fat 5g (Saturated Fat 3.5g; Trans Fat 0g); Cholesterol 25mg; Sodium 180mg; Total Carbohydrate 4g (Dietary Fiber 0g); Protein 3g **Exchanges:** ½ Starch, 1 Fat **Carbohydrate Choices:** 0

> If you are cooking gluten free, always read labels to make sure each recipe ingredient is gluten free. Products and ingredient sources can change.

Pear and Blue Cheese Tart

Prep Time: 20 Minutes • **Start to Finish:** 1 Hour 10 Minutes • 12 servings

CRUST

1½ cups Original Bisquick® mix

⅓ cup hot water

FILLING

2 tablespoons butter

2 shallots, finely chopped (about ⅓ cup)

2 medium pears, peeled, cut into ¼-inch slices (about 2 cups)

¼ cup chopped walnuts

½ cup crumbled blue cheese (2 oz)

2 tablespoons chopped fresh parsley

1 Heat oven to 425°F. Spray 9-inch tart pan with removable bottom with cooking spray.

2 In medium bowl, stir Bisquick mix and hot water until soft dough forms. With fingers dipped in Bisquick mix, press dough in bottom and up side of pan. Bake 10 minutes.

3 Meanwhile, in 8-inch skillet, melt butter over medium heat. Add shallots; cook 2 to 4 minutes, stirring occasionally, until tender. Remove from heat.

4 Arrange pear slices over crust. Spread butter mixture over pears.

5 Bake 20 minutes longer; remove from oven. Sprinkle walnuts over pears. Bake 8 to 10 minutes longer or until tart is golden brown. Immediately sprinkle with cheese. Cool 10 minutes on cooling rack. Sprinkle with parsley. Serve warm or at room temperature.

1 Serving: Calories 130; Total Fat 7g (Saturated Fat 3g; Trans Fat 0.5g); Cholesterol 10mg; Sodium 260mg; Total Carbohydrate 15g (Dietary Fiber 1g); Protein 3g **Exchanges:** 1 Starch, 1 Fat **Carbohydrate Choices:** 1

Substitute 2 medium cooking apples for the pears if you like.

Other blue-veined cheese, such as Gorgonzola or Stilton, can also complement the fruit in this tart.

Two-Cheese Straws

Prep Time: 15 Minutes • **Start to Finish:** 35 Minutes • **36 appetizers**

2½ cups Original Bisquick® mix

⅔ cup milk

½ cup shredded Cheddar cheese (2 oz)

1 tablespoon butter, softened

2 tablespoons grated Parmesan Cheese

Tomato pasta sauce, heated, if desired

1 Heat oven to 400°F. Spray cookie sheets with cooking spray.

2 In large bowl, stir Bisquick mix, milk and Cheddar cheese until soft dough forms. Divide dough in half.

3 On surface lightly sprinkled with Bisquick mix, roll 1 half of dough into 9x6-inch rectangle. Spread with half of the butter. Sprinkle 1 tablespoon of the Parmesan cheese over top. Cut dough lengthwise into 18 (½-inch) strips. Twist each dough strip as many times as possible; place on cookie sheets. Repeat with remaining dough.

4 Bake 6 to 8 minutes or until light golden brown. Serve with pasta sauce.

1 Appetizer: Calories 45; Total Fat 2g (Saturated Fat 1g; Trans Fat 0g); Cholesterol 0mg; Sodium 120mg; Total Carbohydrate 6g (Dietary Fiber 0g); Protein 1g **Exchanges:** ½ Other Carbohydrate, ½ Fat **Carbohydrate Choices:** ½

For a little crunch, sprinkle tops with sesame seed and/or poppy seed before baking.

Savory Tomato-Bacon Biscuit Bites

Prep Time: 30 Minutes • **Start to Finish:** 45 Minutes • 32 appetizers

2 cups Original Bisquick® mix

⅓ cup grated Parmesan cheese

1 tablespoon sugar

1 teaspoon Italian seasoning

¼ teaspoon ground red pepper (cayenne)

⅔ cup mayonnaise

¼ cup milk

4 large plum (Roma) tomatoes, each cut into 8 slices

10 slices bacon, crisply cooked, crumbled

Thinly sliced green onions, if desired

1 Heat oven to 425°F. Lightly spray cookie sheet with cooking spray.

2 In medium bowl, mix Bisquick mix, cheese, sugar, Italian seasoning and red pepper. Add ⅓ cup of the mayonnaise and the milk; stir with fork just until moistened.

3 Place dough on surface sprinkled with Bisquick mix; gently roll in Bisquick mix to coat. Knead 5 to 6 times. Pat or roll dough to ¼-inch thickness. With 1¾-inch round cutter, cut dough into 32 rounds. Place about 1 inch apart on cookie sheet.

4 Bake 8 to 10 minutes or until golden brown. Cool slightly. Spread biscuits with half of remaining ⅓ cup mayonnaise; top each biscuit with tomato slice. Spread tomato slices with remaining mayonnaise; sprinkle evenly with bacon and onions.

1 Appetizer: Calories 86; Total Fat 6g (Saturated Fat 1g; Trans Fat 0g); Cholesterol 0mg; Sodium 203mg; Total Carbohydrate 6g (Dietary Fiber 0g); Protein 2g **Exchanges:** ½ Starch, 1 Fat **Carbohydrate Choices:** ½

Steamed Beef Dumplings

Prep Time: 25 Minutes • **Start to Finish:** 45 Minutes • 30 servings (1 dumpling and 1 teaspoon sauce each)

DUMPLINGS

- 2 tablespoons soy sauce
- 1 teaspoon cornstarch
- 2 medium carrots, shredded (1 cup)
- 2 medium green onions, thinly sliced (2 tablespoons)
- 2 tablespoons chopped fresh cilantro
- ¼ teaspoon salt
- ¾ lb lean (at least 80%) ground beef
- 2 cups Original Bisquick® mix
- ¼ cup boiling water
- 2 tablespoons cold water

SAUCE

- ¼ cup rice vinegar
- ¼ cup soy sauce
- 1 medium green onion, thinly sliced (1 tablespoon)

1 In large bowl, mix 2 tablespoons soy sauce and the cornstarch. Stir in carrots, 2 tablespoons onion, the cilantro and salt. Add beef; mix well. Shape mixture into 30 meatballs, about 1 tablespoon each; set aside.

2 In medium bowl, stir Bisquick mix and boiling water until soft dough forms. Stir in cold water until dough forms a ball (dough will be sticky).

3 Divide dough in half. Return 1 half of dough to bowl; cover and set aside. Divide other half of dough into 15 balls. Place balls on surface sprinkled with Bisquick mix; roll each ball into 3-inch round. Place 1 meatball in center of each dough round. Fold dough up and around meatball, allowing meatball to show at the top. Press dough firmly around meatball, pleating as necessary. Gently flatten bottom of each dumpling. Repeat with remaining dough and meatballs.

4 In 3-quart saucepan, place steamer basket in ½ inch water (water should not touch bottom of basket). Place dumplings, open side up, in basket so edges don't touch. (If all dumplings won't fit in basket, refrigerate remainder until ready to steam.) Cover tightly and heat to boiling; reduce heat to low. Cover; steam dumplings 16 to 18 minutes or until beef is thoroughly cooked and no longer pink in center.

5 Meanwhile, in small bowl, mix vinegar and ¼ cup soy sauce. Sprinkle with 1 tablespoon onion. Serve dumplings warm with sauce.

1 Serving: Calories 60; Total Fat 2.5g (Saturated Fat 1g; Trans Fat 0g); Cholesterol 5mg; Sodium 310mg; Total Carbohydrate 6g (Dietary Fiber 0g); Protein 2g **Exchanges:** ½ Other Carbohydrate, ½ Medium-Fat Meat **Carbohydrate Choices:** ½

> If you don't have a steamer, place the dumplings, open side up, on a greased cookie sheet. Bake at 375°F for 10 to 15 minutes or until beef is thoroughly cooked and no longer pink in center.

Beef Empanaditas

Prep Time: 25 Minutes • **Start to Finish:** 55 Minutes • **20 appetizers**

2 cups Original Bisquick® mix

½ cup hot water

¼ lb lean (at least 80%) ground beef

½ cup chunky-style salsa

1 tablespoon raisins

8 pimiento-stuffed green olives, sliced

½ teaspoon ground cumin

⅛ teaspoon ground cinnamon

1 egg

1 tablespoon water

1 Heat oven to 350°F. Line cookie sheet with cooking parchment paper. In medium bowl, stir Bisquick mix and hot water until stiff dough forms. Let stand 10 minutes.

2 Meanwhile, in 8-inch skillet, cook beef over medium-high heat 5 to 7 minutes, stirring occasionally, until thoroughly cooked; drain. Stir in salsa, raisins, olives, cumin and cinnamon; set aside.

3 Place dough on surface sprinkled with Bisquick mix; gently roll in Bisquick mix to coat. Knead 10 times. Roll dough into 13-inch round, about ⅛ inch thick. With 3-inch round cutter, cut dough into rounds. Gather dough scraps together and reroll; cut into 20 rounds.

4 Spoon 2 to 3 teaspoons beef mixture onto center of each dough round. Fold dough in half over filling; press edges firmly with fork to seal. Place 1 inch apart on cookie sheet.

5 In small bowl, mix egg and 1 tablespoon water until blended. Brush tops of empanaditas with egg mixture. Bake 14 to 16 minutes or until golden brown.

1 Appetizer: Calories 70; Total Fat 2.5g (Saturated Fat 1g; Trans Fat 0g); Cholesterol 15mg; Sodium 220mg; Total Carbohydrate 9g (Dietary Fiber 0g); Protein 2g **Exchanges:** ½ Starch, ½ Fat **Carbohydrate Choices:** ½

Cheesy Bacon Burger Bites

Prep Time: 50 Minutes • **Start to Finish:** 50 Minutes • 28 appetizers

7	slices bacon
28	fancy toothpicks
28	cherry tomatoes
3	leaves romaine lettuce, cut into 28 (1½-inch) pieces
½	cup Original Bisquick® mix
¼	teaspoon salt
¼	teaspoon pepper
1	lb lean (at least 80%) ground beef
1	egg
¼	cup mayonnaise
1	teaspoon Worcestershire sauce
2	oz Cheddar cheese, cut into ¼-inch cubes (about ½ cup)

1 In 10-inch nonstick skillet, cook bacon over medium heat, turning often, until browned but not overly crisp. Drain on paper towels. Reserve 1 tablespoon drippings in skillet. Cut each bacon slice into 4 pieces.

2 Onto each toothpick, thread 1 tomato, 1 bacon piece and 1 lettuce piece; set aside.

3 In large bowl, mix all remaining ingredients except cheese. Fold in cheese. Shape mixture into 28 balls, about 1 tablespoon each; flatten slightly to look like hamburger patties.

4 Heat reserved bacon drippings over medium-high heat. Cook burgers in drippings 4 to 6 minutes, turning once, or until thoroughly cooked and no longer pink in center. Insert 1 toothpick in each burger bite; serve immediately.

1 Appetizer: Calories 70; Total Fat 5g (Saturated Fat 1.5g; Trans Fat 0g); Cholesterol 25mg; Sodium 130mg; Total Carbohydrate 2g (Dietary Fiber 0g); Protein 4g **Exchanges:** ½ Medium-Fat Meat, ½ Fat **Carbohydrate Choices:** 0

Spice up these mini cheeseburgers by using pepper Jack cheese instead of Cheddar and hot pepper sauce instead of Worcestershire sauce.

Serve these burgers with ketchup and mustard for dipping.

Impossibly Easy Bacon Cheeseburger Balls

Prep Time: 20 Minutes • **Start to Finish:** 45 Minutes • 50 servings (2 balls each)

3 cups Original Bisquick® mix

1 lb lean (at least 80%) ground beef

4 cups shredded Cheddar cheese (16 oz)

12 slices bacon, crisply cooked, crumbled (¾ cup)

½ cup grated Parmesan cheese

½ cup milk

¼ cup dill pickle relish

Ketchup and mustard, if desired

1 Heat oven to 350°F. Lightly grease bottom and sides of 15x10x1-inch pan.

2 In large bowl, mix all ingredients except ketchup and mustard, using hands or spoon, until blended. Shape mixture into 50 (1-inch) balls. Place in pan.

3 Bake 20 to 25 minutes or until browned, thoroughly cooked and no longer pink in center. Immediately remove from pan. Serve warm with ketchup and mustard for dipping.

1 Serving: Calories 100; Total Fat 6g (Saturated Fat 3g; Trans Fat 0g); Cholesterol 20mg; Sodium 230mg; Total Carbohydrate 5g (Dietary Fiber 0g); Protein 5g **Exchanges:** ½ Starch, ½ High-Fat Meat, ½ Fat **Carbohydrate Choices:** ½

Use ground turkey in place of the ground beef for a twist on a turkey burger.

To make ahead, prepare as directed through step 2. Cover; refrigerate up to 12 hours. Uncover; bake as directed in step 3.

Chorizo Nuggets with Chimichurri Dipping Sauce

Prep Time: 45 Minutes • **Start to Finish:** 2 Hours 45 Minutes • 48 appetizers

SAUCE

- 1 **bunch fresh parsley (about 1 cup firmly packed)**
- 1 **small onion, cut into fourths**
- 2 **cloves garlic**
- 2 **tablespoons olive oil**
- ¼ **cup white vinegar**
- ½ **teaspoon salt**
- ¼ **cup sour cream**

NUGGETS

- 3 **cups vegetable oil for deep frying**
- 1 **cup plus 2 tablespoons Original Bisquick® mix**
- 1 **package (12 oz) smoked chorizo links, cut into 48 (½-inch) pieces**
- 2 **eggs**
- 1 **cup milk**
- 1 **cup cornmeal**
- 2 **teaspoons ground cumin**
- ½ **teaspoon pepper**

GARNISHES, IF DESIRED

- **Manchego cheese, cubed**
- **Green onions, sliced**
- **Tomato, sliced**
- **Red bell pepper, cut into bite-size pieces**
- **Parsley sprigs**

1 In blender or food processor, place all sauce ingredients except sour cream. Cover; blend on high speed until well blended. Stir in sour cream; cover and refrigerate 2 hours.

2 In 2-quart saucepan, heat 2 to 3 inches oil to 375°F.

3 In medium bowl, place 2 tablespoons of the Bisquick mix; add chorizo, and toss to lightly coat. In another medium bowl, mix eggs, milk, remaining 1 cup Bisquick mix, the cornmeal, cumin and pepper. Dip Bisquick-coated chorizo into batter.

4 Working in batches, fry 4 to 5 chorizo at a time in oil, 3 to 4 minutes, turning once, or until golden brown. Drain on paper towels.

5 Serve on toothpicks with garnishes and sauce.

1 Appetizer: Calories 90; Total Fat 6g (Saturated Fat 2g; Trans Fat 0g); Cholesterol 15mg; Sodium 150mg; Total Carbohydrate 5g (Dietary Fiber 0g); Protein 2g **Exchanges:** ½ Starch, 1 Fat **Carbohydrate Choices:** ½

Chimichurri originated in Argentina as a sauce or marinade for grilled meats. It is typically served as an accompaniment.

Cilantro can be used in place of the parsley in this recipe.

Cheesy Chorizo Bites with Salsa Dip

Prep Time: 20 Minutes • **Start to Finish:** 45 Minutes • **40 appetizers**

DIP

- 1 package (8 oz) cream cheese, softened
- ½ cup sour cream
- 2 teaspoons Mexican seasoning
- 1 cup medium salsa

BITES

- 3 cups Original Bisquick® mix
- 1 tablespoon Mexican seasoning
- 1 cup shredded Cheddar cheese (4 oz), chopped
- 1 lb bulk chorizo sausage, crumbled, cooked, drained and cooled
- 1 can (14.75 oz) cream-style sweet corn
- ¼ cup milk
- 40 small pitted black olives, drained (from 6-oz can)

1 In small bowl, beat cream cheese and sour cream with electric mixer on low speed 30 seconds, scraping bowl constantly, until mixture is smooth. Add 2 teaspoons seasoning and the salsa; beat until blended. Cover; refrigerate until ready to serve.

2 Heat oven to 450°F. Line 2 large cookie sheets with cooking parchment paper.

3 In large bowl, mix Bisquick mix and 1 tablespoon seasoning. Stir in Cheddar cheese and chorizo; mix well. In small bowl, mix corn and milk. Stir corn mixture into Bisquick mixture until well combined.

4 Onto cookie sheets, drop chorizo mixture evenly into 40 mounds (about 2 tablespoons each). Press 1 olive into center of each mound, sealing it inside.

5 Bake 12 to 13 minutes or until golden brown. Serve nuggets with dip.

1 Appetizer: Calories 140; Total Fat 9g (Saturated Fat 4g; Trans Fat 0g); Cholesterol 20mg; Sodium 430mg; Total Carbohydrate 9g (Dietary Fiber 0g); Protein 5g **Exchanges:** ½ Starch, ½ Lean Meat, 1½ Fat **Carbohydrate Choices:** ½

Cheesy Chorizo Bites with Salsa Dip is a 2013 Bisquick Family Favorites Recipe Contest award-winning recipe developed by Alberta Dunbar, 1st Place, San Diego County Fair (CA).

The dip can be made the day before and served warm or cold.

Cornmeal-Coated Chicken Bites

Prep Time: 15 Minutes • **Start to Finish:** 35 Minutes • **48 servings (1 chicken bite and about 1 teaspoon sauce each)**

¼ cup butter, melted

1 cup Original Bisquick® mix

½ cup cornmeal

1 teaspoon seasoned salt

¼ cup milk

1 egg

4 boneless skinless chicken breasts, cut into 48 (1-inch) pieces

1 cup barbecue sauce, heated

1 Heat oven to 425°F. In 15x10x1-inch pan, pour 2 tablespoons of the melted butter.

2 In large resealable food-storage plastic bag, mix Bisquick mix, cornmeal and seasoned salt. In medium bowl, beat milk and egg with whisk until blended.

3 Working in batches, dip 6 chicken pieces in milk mixture; place in bag of Bisquick mixture. Seal bag; shake to coat. Place on cookie sheet. Repeat with remaining chicken pieces. Drizzle remaining 2 tablespoons melted butter over coated chicken pieces.

4 Bake 12 minutes. Turn; bake 7 to 8 minutes longer or until golden brown and chicken is no longer pink in center. Serve with barbecue sauce.

1 Serving: Calories 45; Total Fat 2g (Saturated Fat 1g; Trans Fat 0g); Cholesterol 15mg; Sodium 130mg; Total Carbohydrate 5g (Dietary Fiber 0g); Protein 3g **Exchanges:** ½ Very Lean Meat, ½ Fat **Carbohydrate Choices:** ½

Buffalo Chicken Bites with Blue Cheese Dipping Sauce

Prep Time: 25 Minutes • **Start to Finish:** 55 Minutes • **40 appetizers**

BITES

- 1 **egg white**
- ⅓ **cup hot Buffalo wing sauce**
- 1 **lb boneless skinless chicken breasts, cut into 40 (1-inch) pieces**
- ¾ **cup Original Bisquick® mix**
- 3 **tablespoons cornmeal**
- 1 **teaspoon salt**
- ½ **teaspoon pepper**
  Vegetable oil for frying

SAUCE

- ¾ **cup crumbled blue cheese (3 oz)**
- 6 **tablespoons sour cream**
- 6 **tablespoons light mayonnaise**
- 3 **tablespoons milk**

1 In medium bowl, mix egg white and Buffalo wing sauce. Stir in chicken. Cover; refrigerate 30 minutes.

2 Line cookie sheet with waxed paper. In large resealable food-storage plastic bag, mix Bisquick mix, cornmeal, salt and pepper. With slotted spoon, remove one-quarter of the chicken pieces from bowl; place in bag of Bisquick mixture. Seal bag; shake to coat. Shake excess Bisquick mixture from chicken; place on cookie sheet. Repeat with remaining chicken.

3 In small bowl, mix sauce ingredients until blended. Cover; refrigerate until serving time.

4 In 10-inch nonstick skillet, heat ¼ inch oil over medium-high heat 2 to 4 minutes or until hot (350°F). Working in batches, cook chicken bites in oil, 3 to 4 minutes, turning once, or until golden brown. Drain on paper towels. Serve chicken with sauce.

1 Appetizer: Calories 60; Total Fat 4g (Saturated Fat 1.5g; Trans Fat 0g); Cholesterol 10mg; Sodium 210mg; Total Carbohydrate 3g (Dietary Fiber 0g); Protein 3g **Exchanges:** ½ Lean Meat, ½ Fat **Carbohydrate Choices:** 0

The chicken bites can be breaded ahead of time. Prepare through step 2; refrigerate until ready to cook.

Turn this appetizer into a great salad. Serve chicken bites over chopped lettuce and tomatoes with the dipping sauce as the dressing.

Hot and Spicy Chicken Wings

Prep Time: 15 Minutes • **Start to Finish:** 5 Hours 5 Minutes • **24 appetizers**

1 cup red pepper sauce

1 teaspoon garlic salt

24 chicken wing drummettes

2 tablespoons butter

1 cup Original Bisquick® mix

¾ teaspoon onion salt

½ teaspoon black pepper

¼ teaspoon ground red pepper (cayenne)

Ranch or blue cheese dressing

1 In large bowl, mix pepper sauce and garlic salt until blended. Add chicken; toss to coat. Cover; refrigerate at least 4 hours but no longer than 24 hours.

2 Heat oven to 450°F. In 15x10x1-inch pan, melt butter in oven.

3 In medium bowl, mix Bisquick mix, onion salt, black pepper and red pepper. Remove chicken from sauce; discard sauce. Coat chicken with Bisquick mixture. Place in single layer in pan.

4 Bake uncovered 25 minutes. Turn; bake 20 to 25 minutes longer or until chicken is golden brown and juice of chicken is clear when thickest part is cut to bone (at least 165°F). Serve with dressing.

1 Appetizer: Calories 80; Total Fat 5g (Saturated Fat 2g; Trans Fat 0g); Cholesterol 20mg; Sodium 420mg; Total Carbohydrate 4g (Dietary Fiber 0g); Protein 5g **Exchanges:** ½ Starch, ½ Lean Meat, ½ Fat **Carbohydrate Choices:** 0

Marinades add flavor and help tenderize meats and poultry. Letting chicken marinate more than 24 hours, however, will cause it to break down, resulting in mushy chicken with an overpowering flavor.

Line the baking pan with foil before you melt the butter. When the wings are done, just throw away the foil—no dirty pan!

Super-Easy, Super-Versatile Chicken Fingers

Fresh, fast, homemade—and BAKED, not fried—Bisquick helps you make fabulous chicken fingers in about 30 minutes. This recipie will serve four as a main dish or six to eight as an appetizer.

Ultimate Chicken Fingers

Prep Time: 15 Minutes • **Start to Finish:** 30 Minutes • 4 servings

3 boneless skinless chicken breasts (1 lb), cut crosswise into ½-inch strips

⅔ cup Original Bisquick® mix

½ cup grated Parmesan cheese

½ teaspoon salt or garlic salt

½ teaspoon paprika

1 egg, slightly beaten

3 tablespoons butter, melted

1 Heat oven to 450°F. Line cookie sheet with foil; spray with cooking spray.

2 In 1-gallon resealable food-storage plastic bag, place Bisquick mix, cheese, salt and paprika. Seal bag; shake to blend.

3 Dip half of the chicken strips in egg; place in bag. Seal bag; shake to coat. Place chicken on cookie sheet. Repeat with remaining chicken and Bisquick mixture. Drizzle butter over chicken.

4 Bake 12 to 14 minutes, turning after 6 minutes, until chicken is no longer pink in center.

1 Serving: Calories 340; Total Fat 19g (Saturated Fat 9g; Trans Fat 1g); Cholesterol 140mg; Sodium 930mg; Total Carbohydrate 13g (Dietary Fiber 0g); Protein 28g **Exchanges:** 1 Starch, 3½ Very Lean Meat, 3 Fat **Carbohydrate Choices:** 1

To make these chicken fingers your own, try one of these variations. Then see page 54 for delicious homemade sauces to try too.

To make Bacon-Cheddar Chicken Fingers, substitute finely shredded Cheddar cheese for the Parmesan cheese, and add ¼ cup cooked real bacon bits with the cheese.

To make Crunchy Honey-Roasted Chicken Fingers, substitute ⅓ cup finely chopped honey-roasted or dry-roasted peanuts for the Parmesan cheese. Omit paprika.

To make Taco Night Chicken Fingers, substitute 1 package (1 ounce) taco seasoning mix for the cheese, salt and paprika.

To make Italian Chicken Fingers, increase Bisquick mix to 1⅓ cups. Omit cheese, salt and paprika. Add 1 teaspoon Italian seasoning with the Bisquick mix.

Dipping Sauces

Create a winning combo by serving up a ready-made sauce or quick-to-mix-up dip for your chicken fingers.

Sriracha Dipping Sauce:
Mix ½ cup mayonnaise and 1 tablespoon Sriracha sauce or buffalo wing sauce.

Bacon-Ranch Dipping Sauce: Mix ½ cup ranch dressing with 2 tablespoons cooked real bacon bits or pieces (from a 3-ounce bag).

Honey Mustard Dipping Sauce: In small bowl, mix ¼ cup honey and 1½ tablespoons Dijon or yellow mustard.

Creamy Honey Dipping Sauce: In small bowl, mix ¼ cup mayonnaise or sour cream with 2 tablespoons honey.

Salsa–Sour Cream Dipping Sauce: In small bowl, mix ¼ cup chunky-style salsa and ¼ cup sour cream.

Honey

Creamy Honey
Dipping Sauce

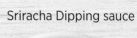
Sriracha Dipping sauce

Bacon-Ranch Dipping
Sauce

Sweet-and-sour sauce

Salsa

Salsa–Sour Cream
Dipping Sauce

Barbecue sauce

Buffalo wing sauce

Honey Mustard Dipping Sauce

Gluten-Free Ultimate Chicken Fingers

Prep Time: 25 Minutes • **Start to Finish:** 25 Minutes • 5 servings

¾ cup Bisquick® Gluten Free mix

½ cup grated Parmesan cheese

1 teaspoon paprika

½ teaspoon salt or garlic salt

2 eggs

3 boneless skinless chicken breasts (1 lb), cut crosswise into ½-inch strips

3 tablespoons butter, melted

1 Heat oven to 450°F. Line cookie sheet with foil; spray with cooking spray (without flour).

2 In shallow dish, mix Bisquick mix, cheese, paprika and salt. In another shallow dish, beat eggs slightly.

3 Dip chicken strips into eggs, then coat with Bisquick mixture. Repeat dipping coated chicken in eggs and Bisquick mixture. Place chicken on cookie sheet. Drizzle butter over chicken.

4 Bake 12 to 14 minutes, turning after 6 minutes, until chicken is no longer pink in center.

1 Serving: Calories 310; Total Fat 15g (Saturated Fat 8g; Trans Fat 0g); Cholesterol 165mg; Sodium 740mg; Total Carbohydrate 16g (Dietary Fiber 0g); Protein 28g **Exchanges:** 1 Starch, 3½ Lean Meat, 1 Fat **Carbohydrate Choices:** 1

If you are cooking gluten free, always read labels to make sure each recipe ingredient is gluten free. Products and ingredient sources can change.

Fried Chicken and Waffle Sandwich Bites

Prep Time: 1 Hour 30 Minutes • **Start to Finish:** 1 Hour 30 Minutes • 16 appetizers

BACON AND CHICKEN

- 8 slices bacon, each cut in half
- 2 boneless skinless chicken breasts (4 oz each)
- ⅛ teaspoon salt

  Dash freshly ground black pepper
- ½ cup Original Bisquick® mix
- ½ teaspoon chipotle chile powder
- 1 egg
- 2 tablespoons vegetable oil

BUTTER

- ¼ cup butter, softened
- 2 tablespoons pure maple syrup
- 2 teaspoons bourbon

WAFFLES

- 1¼ cups Original Bisquick® mix
- 1 egg
- ¾ cup regular or nonalcoholic beer (6 oz)
- 1 tablespoon vegetable oil

1 In 12-inch skillet, cook bacon over low heat 8 to 10 minutes, turning occasionally, until crisp. Drain on paper towels; set aside.

2 Between pieces of plastic wrap or waxed paper, place each chicken breast smooth side down; gently pound with flat side of meat mallet or rolling pin until about ½ inch thick. Cut into 16 (2-inch) pieces. Season chicken with salt and pepper.

3 In shallow bowl, mix ½ cup Bisquick mix and the chile powder. In another small bowl, beat egg with fork. Dip chicken into egg mixture; coat with Bisquick mixture.

4 In 12-inch nonstick skillet, heat 2 tablespoons oil over medium heat. Add chicken; cook 6 to 8 minutes, turning once, until golden brown and chicken is no longer pink in center.

5 Meanwhile, in another small bowl, stir butter ingredients until smooth. Set aside.

6 Heat waffle maker. (Waffle makers without nonstick coating may need to be brushed with vegetable oil or sprayed with cooking spray before batter for each waffle is added.) In medium bowl, stir waffle ingredients until blended. For each waffle, spoon about 1 tablespoon batter onto center of each quarter of waffle maker. Close lid of waffle maker.

7 Bake about 2 minutes or until steaming stops and waffle is golden brown. Carefully remove waffles. Repeat with remaining batter, making 32 small waffles. For each sandwich bite, spread about 1 teaspoon butter on each of 16 waffles. Top with 1 half slice bacon, 1 piece chicken and another waffle. Serve immediately.

1 Appetizer: Calories 160; Total Fat 10g (Saturated Fat 3.5g; Trans Fat 0.5g); Cholesterol 45mg; Sodium 320mg; Total Carbohydrate 11g (Dietary Fiber 0g); Protein 6g **Exchanges:** ½ Starch, ½ Lean Meat, 2 Fat **Carbohydrate Choices:** 1

Peppered Pork with Pecan Biscuits

Prep Time: 15 Minutes • **Start to Finish:** 1 Hour • **60 sandwiches**

2 (1 lb) pork tenderloins

2 teaspoons pepper

1 teaspoon salt

1 package fast-acting dry yeast

1 tablespoon sugar

¾ cup warm water (105°F to 115°F)

1 box (20 oz) Original Bisquick® mix

½ cup chopped pecans

1 cup buttermilk

¼ cup butter, melted

2 tablespoons refrigerated basil pesto

½ cup all-purpose flour

⅔ cup country-style Dijon mustard

1 Heat oven to 450°F. Lightly grease rack of roasting pan with vegetable oil or shortening. Rub pork with pepper and salt; place on rack in roasting pan.

2 Roast 20 to 25 minutes or until pork has slight blush of pink in center and meat thermometer inserted in center reads 145°F. Remove from oven; let stand 10 minutes. Cut into thin slices; cover to keep warm. Reduce oven temperature to 425°F.

3 Meanwhile, lightly spray cookie sheets with cooking spray. In large bowl, mix yeast, sugar and warm water; let stand 5 minutes. Add Bisquick mix, pecans, buttermilk, butter and pesto to yeast mixture; stir just until moistened. Stir in flour as needed (up to ½ cup) until dough pulls away from side of bowl.

4 Place dough on lightly floured surface; gently knead 2 to 3 times. Pat or roll dough to 1-inch thickness. With 1½-inch round cutter, cut dough into 60 rounds. Place biscuits on cookie sheets.

5 Bake 10 to 12 minutes or until lightly browned. Split biscuits in half; top bottom half of biscuits with sliced pork, mustard and top half of biscuit.

1 Sandwich: Calories 77; Total Fat 4g (Saturated Fat 1g; Trans Fat 0g); Cholesterol 0mg; Sodium 178mg; Total Carbohydrate 8g (Dietary Fiber 0g); Protein 4g **Exchanges:** ½ Starch, ½ Lean Meat, ½ Fat **Carbohydrate Choices:** ½

Antipasto Pizzettes

Prep Time: 30 Minutes • **Start to Finish:** 40 Minutes • **24 appetizers**

2 cups Original Bisquick® mix

½ cup water

2 tablespoons olive or vegetable oil

2 teaspoons dried basil leaves

½ cup shredded mozzarella cheese (2 oz)

¼ cup basil pesto

24 slices plum (Roma) tomatoes (about 3 small)

24 slices pepperoni

24 slices pickled banana peppers or pepperoncini peppers (bottled Italian peppers), if desired

1 Heat oven to 450°F. Lightly spray cookie sheet with cooking spray.

2 In medium bowl, stir Bisquick mix, water, oil and 1 teaspoon of the basil until soft dough forms. Place dough on surface sprinkled with Bisquick mix; gently roll in Bisquick mix to coat. Knead 10 times.

3 Roll dough into 12-inch round, about ¼ inch thick. With 2-inch round cutter, cut dough into rounds. Gather dough scraps together and reroll; cut into 24 rounds. Place 1 inch apart on cookie sheet.

4 Bake 8 to 10 minutes or until light golden brown. Cool completely, about 15 minutes. Store in airtight container until serving.

5 Meanwhile, in small bowl, mix cheese and remaining 1 teaspoon basil. To serve, spread about ½ teaspoon pesto on each biscuit round. Top each with 1 slice tomato, 1 slice pepperoni and about 1 teaspoon cheese mixture. Top each with 1 slice banana pepper. Serve at room temperature.

1 Appetizer: Calories 100; Total Fat 7g (Saturated Fat 2g; Trans Fat 0g); Cholesterol 5mg; Sodium 290mg; Total Carbohydrate 7g (Dietary Fiber 0g); Protein 3g **Exchanges:** ½ Starch, 1½ Fat **Carbohydrate Choices:** ½

Bake and freeze the biscuit rounds up to 1 week ahead of time. Heat thawed rounds on a cookie sheet in the oven at 450°F for 2 to 4 minutes.

Tuna Appetizer Pizza

Prep Time: 20 Minutes • **Start to Finish:** 2 Hours 30 Minutes • 40 appetizers

1½ cups Original Bisquick® mix

⅓ cup boiling water

2 tablespoons sliced green onions

1 package (8 oz) cream cheese, softened

½ cup sour cream

1 teaspoon dried dill weed

⅛ teaspoon garlic powder

1 can (5 oz) tuna, drained

3 cups fresh vegetables, such as sliced mushrooms, cherry tomato halves, chopped broccoli

1 cup shredded Cheddar or Swiss cheese (4 oz)

1 Heat oven to 450°F. In medium bowl, stir Bisquick mix, boiling water and onions until soft dough forms; beat vigorously 20 strokes.

2 Using hands coated with Bisquick mix, pat dough into ungreased 12-inch pizza pan, forming ½-inch rim.

3 Bake 9 to 10 minutes or until light brown. Cool 10 minutes.

4 In medium bowl, stir cream cheese, sour cream, dill weed, garlic powder and tuna until smooth; spread evenly over crust. Refrigerate 1 to 2 hours or until chilled. Just before serving, top with vegetables and cheese. Cut into 40 bite-size wedges.

1 Appetizer: Calories 60; Total Fat 4g (Saturated Fat 2.5g; Trans Fat 0g); Cholesterol 10mg; Sodium 130mg; Total Carbohydrate 3g (Dietary Fiber 0g); Protein 2g **Exchanges:** ½ Lean Meat, ½ Fat **Carbohydrate Choices:** 0

CHAPTER 2

Warm-from-the-Oven Breads

Mexican Chocolate Doughnut Holes

Prep Time: 25 Minutes • **Start to Finish:** 25 Minutes • 38 doughnut holes

DOUGHNUT HOLES

Oil for deep frying

2 cups Original Bisquick® mix

2 tablespoons sugar

¼ teaspoon ground nutmeg

¼ cup milk

1 teaspoon vanilla

1 egg, beaten

COATING

½ cup sugar

2¾ teaspoons unsweetened baking cocoa

½ teaspoon ground cinnamon

1 In deep fryer or 2-quart heavy saucepan, heat 2 to 3 inches oil to 375°F.

2 In brown-paper lunch bag (about 10¾x5 inches) or medium bowl, place all coating ingredients.

3 In medium bowl, stir all doughnut hole ingredients, except oil, just until soft dough forms. Place half of dough in small bowl; cover and refrigerate. Shape remaining dough into 19 (1-inch) balls (if dough is sticky, dip fingers in Bisquick mix).

4 Carefully place balls, 5 or 6 at a time, into hot oil. Fry 1 to 2 minutes or until golden brown all around; drain on paper towels. Immediately, place 2 or 3 doughnut holes at a time in bag; shake gently to coat with sugar mixture or gently roll in coating in bowl. Repeat with refrigerated dough.

1 Doughnut Hole: Calories 80; Total Fat 6g (Saturated Fat 1g; Trans Fat 0g); Cholesterol 5mg; Sodium 80mg; Total Carbohydrate 8g (Dietary Fiber 0g); Protein 0g **Exchanges:** ½ Other Carbohydrate, 1 Fat **Carbohydrate Choices:** ½

If the cooking oil is too hot, the exterior of the doughnuts browns too quickly and the interior will be undercooked. If the oil is too cool, the doughnuts become saturated with oil before they are fully cooked and will taste greasy.

To make Butterscotch Doughnut Holes, use 2 boxes (4-serving size) butterscotch instant pudding and pie filling mix (dry) in place of the coating. Prepare doughnut holes as directed.

To make Cookies & Cream Doughnut Holes, use 5 creme-filled chocolate sandwich cookies, crushed, mixed with ½ cup powdered sugar in place of the coating. Prepare doughnut holes as directed.

Gluten-Free Baked Orange-Cardamom Doughnuts

Prep Time: 30 Minutes • **Start to Finish:** 45 Minutes • **12 doughnuts**

DOUGHNUTS

- ½ cup butter, softened
- ¼ cup granulated sugar
- 2 eggs
- ¾ cup buttermilk
- 1 teaspoon grated orange peel
- 2 tablespoons orange juice
- 2 cups Bisquick® Gluten Free mix
- 1 teaspoon ground cardamom or cinnamon

GLAZE

- 2 cups powdered sugar
- 6 tablespoons butter, melted
- 1 teaspoon grated orange peel
- 2 to 3 tablespoons orange juice

1 Heat oven to 425°F. Lightly grease 2 (6-count) doughnut pans.

2 In medium bowl, beat ½ cup butter, the granulated sugar and eggs with whisk until smooth. Add buttermilk, orange peel and orange juice; beat until well blended. Stir in Bisquick mix and cardamom just until moistened (batter will be thick).

3 Spoon batter evenly into doughnut pans, filling each well about ¼-inch from top of pan.

4 Bake 6 to 8 minutes or until toothpick inserted in center comes out clean. Cool 5 minutes. Remove doughnuts from pan to cooling rack. Cool 15 minutes.

5 Meanwhile, in medium bowl, stir all glaze ingredients until smooth and glaze consistency. Dip rounded sides of doughnuts in glaze. Let stand until set.

1 Doughnut: Calories 280; Total Fat 15g (Saturated Fat 9g; Trans Fat 0.5g); Cholesterol 70mg; Sodium 370mg; Total Carbohydrate 33g (Dietary Fiber 0g); Protein 3g **Exchanges:** 1 Starch, 1 Other Carbohydrate, 3 Fat **Carbohydrate Choices:** 2

If you are cooking gluten free, always read labels to make sure each recipe ingredient is gluten free. Products and ingredient sources can change.

If you don't have buttermilk on hand, mix 1½ teaspoons white vinegar or lemon juice in ¾ cup milk. Let stand 5 minutes.

Double-Berry Doughnuts

Prep Time: 25 Minutes • **Start to Finish:** 1 Hour • **12 doughnuts**

2 cups Original Bisquick® mix

¼ cup granulated sugar

⅔ cup milk

2½ teaspoons vanilla

1 egg

½ cup dried blueberries

½ cup frozen raspberries (do not thaw)

2 tablespoons water

2 cups powdered sugar

4½ teaspoons milk

1 Heat oven to 425°F. Lightly grease 2 (6-count) doughnut pans.

2 In medium bowl, stir Bisquick mix, 2 tablespoons of the granulated sugar, ⅔ cup milk, 2 teaspoons of the vanilla and the egg until blended. Stir in blueberries. Spoon batter into large resealable food-storage plastic bag; seal bag. Cut off ½-inch corner of bag. Squeeze bag to pipe batter into pans.

3 Bake 7 to 9 minutes or until toothpick inserted near center comes out clean. Immediately remove doughnuts from pan to cooling rack. Cool completely.

4 In 1-quart saucepan, heat raspberries, water and remaining 2 tablespoons granulated sugar to boiling over medium heat. Cook 2 to 3 minutes or until thickened and syrup consistency. Strain; cool. Stir in 1 cup of the powdered sugar and remaining ½ teaspoon vanilla with whisk until smooth and thickened. Dip tops of doughnuts into berry glaze; let excess drip off. Return to cooling rack. Let stand until set.

5 In medium bowl, mix remaining 1 cup powdered sugar and 4½ teaspoons milk with whisk until smooth. Drizzle over doughnuts. Let stand until set.

1 Doughnut: Calories 230; Total Fat 3.5g (Saturated Fat 1g; Trans Fat 0g); Cholesterol 0mg; Sodium 260mg; Total Carbohydrate 48g (Dietary Fiber 2g); Protein 3g **Exchanges:** 1 Starch, 2 Other Carbohydrate, ½ Fat **Carbohydrate Choices:** 3

Caramel Pretzel Doughnuts

Prep Time: 20 Minutes • **Start to Finish:** 45 Minutes • **12 doughnuts**

⅓ cup butter

⅔ cup packed brown sugar

¼ cup milk

2 cups Original Bisquick® mix

2 tablespoons granulated sugar

⅔ cup milk

1 teaspoon vanilla

1 egg

2 tablespoons butter, melted

½ cup powdered sugar

1 cup small pretzel twists, broken

⅓ cup coconut

1 Heat oven to 425°F. Lightly grease 2 (6-count) doughnut pans.

2 In 2-quart saucepan, melt ⅓ cup butter over medium heat. Stir in brown sugar. Heat to boiling, stirring constantly. Stir in 3 tablespoons of the milk; return to boiling. Remove from heat; cool to room temperature.

3 Meanwhile, in medium bowl, stir Bisquick mix, granulated sugar, ⅔ cup milk, the vanilla and egg until blended. Stir in melted butter. Spoon batter into large resealable food-storage plastic bag; seal bag. Cut off ½-inch corner of bag. Squeeze bag to pipe batter into pans.

4 Bake 7 to 9 minutes or until toothpick inserted near center comes out clean. Immediately remove doughnuts from pan to cooling rack; cool completely.

5 Gradually beat powdered sugar into brown sugar mixture with whisk until smooth, adding remaining 1 tablespoon milk, if needed. Glaze doughnuts; sprinkle with pretzels and coconut.

1 Doughnut: Calories 260; Total Fat 11g (Saturated Fat 6g; Trans Fat 0g); Cholesterol 0mg; Sodium 410mg; Total Carbohydrate 39g (Dietary Fiber 0g); Protein 3g **Exchanges:** 1 Starch, 1½ Other Carbohydrate, 2 Fat **Carbohydrate Choices:** 2½

Black and Orange Doughnuts

Prep Time: 15 Minutes • **Start to Finish:** 40 Minutes • 12 doughnuts

2 cups Original Bisquick® mix

2 tablespoons sugar

⅔ cup milk

1 teaspoon vanilla

1 egg

2 tablespoons butter, melted

⅔ cup crushed creme-filled chocolate sandwich cookies

4 oz semisweet baking chocolate, chopped

½ cup whipping cream

2 tablespoons orange candy sprinkles

⅓ cup coarsely crushed creme-filled chocolate sandwich cookies

1 Heat oven to 425°F. Lightly grease 2 (6-count) doughnut pans.

2 In medium bowl, stir Bisquick mix, sugar, milk, vanilla and egg until blended. Stir in melted butter. Stir in ⅔ cup crushed cookies. Spoon batter into large resealable food-storage plastic bag; seal bag. Cut off ½-inch corner of bag. Squeeze bag to pipe batter into pans.

3 Bake 7 to 9 minutes or until toothpick inserted near center comes out clean. Remove doughnuts from pan to cooling rack. Cool 5 minutes.

4 In small microwavable bowl, microwave chocolate and whipping cream uncovered on High 45 seconds; stir with whisk until smooth. Dip tops of doughnuts into chocolate mixture; let excess drip off. Return to cooling rack. Decorate with candy sprinkles and coarsely crushed cookies. Let stand until set.

1 Doughnut: Calories 260; Total Fat 14g (Saturated Fat 6g; Trans Fat 0g); Cholesterol 0mg; Sodium 350mg; Total Carbohydrate 33g (Dietary Fiber 1g); Protein 4g **Exchanges:** 1 Starch, 1 Other Carbohydrate, 2½ Fat **Carbohydrate Choices:** 2

Cinnamon-Sugar Pinwheels

Prep Time: 20 Minutes • **Start to Finish:** 40 Minutes • 12 pinwheels

PINWHEELS

2¼ cups Original Bisquick® mix

½ cup milk

1 tablespoon butter, softened

¼ cup granulated sugar

1 teaspoon ground cinnamon

½ cup finely chopped walnuts

½ cup dried currants

1 tablespoon butter, melted

GLAZE

¾ cup powdered sugar

¼ teaspoon vanilla

3 teaspoons milk

1 Heat oven to 400°F. Line cookie sheet with cooking parchment paper.

2 In medium bowl, stir Bisquick mix and ½ cup milk until soft dough forms. Place dough on surface generously sprinkled with Bisquick mix; roll in Bisquick mix to coat. Knead 5 times.

3 Pat or roll dough into 11x8-inch rectangle. Spread with 1 table-spoon softened butter. In small bowl, mix granulated sugar, cinnamon, walnuts and currants; sprinkle over dough, pressing in slightly. Starting with long side, roll up dough tightly; seal edge. Cut into ¾-inch slices. Place slices about 1 inch apart on cookie sheet. Brush with melted butter.

4 Bake 8 to 10 minutes or until golden brown. Remove pinwheels from cookie sheet to cooling rack. Cool 10 minutes.

5 Meanwhile, in small bowl, mix powdered sugar, vanilla and 3 teaspoons milk, 1 teaspoon at a time, until glaze is thin enough to drizzle.

6 Drizzle glaze over pinwheels. Serve warm.

1 Pinwheel: Calories 210; Total Fat 8g (Saturated Fat 2.5g; Trans Fat 1g); Cholesterol 5mg; Sodium 290mg; Total Carbohydrate 32g (Dietary Fiber 1g); Protein 3g **Exchanges:** 1 Starch, 1 Other Carbohydrate, 1½ Fat **Carbohydrate Choices:** 2

Cherry–Chocolate Chip Scones

Prep Time: 20 Minutes • **Start to Finish:** 35 Minutes • 8 scones

2 cups Original Bisquick® mix

⅓ cup finely chopped dried cherries

⅓ cup miniature semisweet chocolate chips

3 tablespoons granulated sugar

⅓ cup whipping cream

1 egg

1 tablespoon milk

1 tablespoon coarse sugar

1 Heat oven to 425°F. Grease cookie sheet with shortening.

2 In large bowl, stir Bisquick mix, cherries, chocolate chips, 3 tablespoons granulated sugar, the whipping cream and egg until soft dough forms.

3 Place dough on surface sprinkled with Bisquick mix; gently roll in Bisquick mix to coat. Knead 10 times.

4 On cookie sheet, pat dough into 8-inch round. Brush dough with milk; sprinkle with 1 tablespoon coarse sugar. Using sharp knife, cut round into 8 wedges, but do not separate.

5 Bake 12 to 15 minutes or until golden brown. Carefully separate wedges with knife; remove from cookie sheet to cooling rack. Serve warm.

1 Scone: Calories 250; Total Fat 10g (Saturated Fat 5g; Trans Fat 1.5g); Cholesterol 40mg; Sodium 380mg; Total Carbohydrate 36g (Dietary Fiber 1g); Protein 3g **Exchanges:** 1 Starch, 1½ Other Carbohydrate, 1½ Fat **Carbohydrate Choices:** 2½

> **Pick your favorite fruit!** Dried apricots, cranberries and blueberries are great stand-ins for the dried cherries.

Chocolate Chip Scones

Prep Time: 15 Minutes • **Start to Finish:** 35 Minutes • 12 scones

3 cups Bisquick Heart Smart® mix

¼ cup sugar

½ teaspoon ground cinnamon

2 tablespoons cold butter

⅔ cup fat-free half-and-half

2 tablespoons miniature semisweet chocolate chips

1 egg, separated

1 tablespoon fat-free half-and-half

1 tablespoon sugar

1 Heat oven to 400°F. Line cookie sheet with foil.

2 In large bowl, mix Bisquick mix, ¼ cup of the sugar and the cinnamon. Cut in butter, using pastry blender or fork, until mixture looks like coarse crumbs. Add ⅔ cup half-and-half, the chocolate chips and egg white; stir just until moistened.

3 Onto cookie sheet, drop dough by ¼ cupfuls to make 12 scones; place in freezer for 5 minutes. In small bowl, beat egg yolk and 1 tablespoon half-and-half; brush over tops of scones. Sprinkle with remaining 1 tablespoon sugar.

4 Bake 11 to 13 minutes or until golden brown. Immediately remove scones from cookie sheet to cooling rack. Serve warm.

1 Scone: Calories 191; Total Fat 5g (Saturated Fat 2g; Trans Fat 0g); Cholesterol 0mg; Sodium 361mg; Total Carbohydrate 35g (Dietary Fiber 1g); Protein 3g **Exchanges:** 1½ Starch, 1 Other Carbohydrate, ½ Fat **Carbohydrate Choices:** 2½

White Chocolate–Cranberry Scones

Prep Time: 20 Minutes • **Start to Finish:** 40 Minutes • 18 scones

3 cups Original Bisquick® mix

½ cup granulated sugar

½ cup cold butter

1 cup white vanilla baking chips (6 oz)

1 cup sweetened dried cranberries

1 teaspoon finely grated orange peel

½ cup whipping cream

1 egg

1 tablespoon whipping cream

2 tablespoons coarse sugar or 1 tablespoon granulated sugar

1 Heat oven to 400°F. In large bowl, mix Bisquick mix and ½ cup granulated sugar. Cut in butter, using pastry blender or fork, until mixture looks like fine crumbs. Stir in baking chips, cranberries and orange peel. In small bowl, mix ½ cup whipping cream and the egg until blended. Stir into crumb mixture until dough forms.

2 Place dough on surface lightly sprinkled with Bisquick mix; gently roll in Bisquick mix to coat. Knead 3 to 4 times. Pat or roll dough to ¾-inch thickness. With 2-inch round cutter dipped in Bisquick mix, cut dough into 18 rounds.

3 On ungreased cookie sheet, place rounds 1 inch apart. Brush rounds with 1 tablespoon whipping cream; sprinkle with coarse sugar.

4 Bake 16 to 19 minutes or until light golden brown. Immediately remove from cookie sheet to cooling rack. Serve warm.

1 Scone: Calories 270; Total Fat 14g (Saturated Fat 8g; Trans Fat 0g); Cholesterol 0mg; Sodium 320mg; Total Carbohydrate 34g (Dietary Fiber 0g); Protein 3g **Exchanges:** 1 Starch, 1 Other Carbohydrate, 2½ Fat **Carbohydrate Choices:** 2

Pear-Walnut Scones

Prep Time: 20 Minutes • **Start to Finish:** 40 Minutes • 8 scones

2 cups Original Bisquick® mix

¼ cup granulated sugar

½ cup whipping cream

1 egg, slightly beaten

¾ cup chopped unpeeled red Bartlett pear

½ cup chopped walnuts, toasted*

1 tablespoon coarse sugar

8 walnut halves

1 Heat oven to 425°F. Lightly spray cookie sheet with cooking spray.

2 In medium bowl, mix Bisquick mix and granulated sugar. Stir in whipping cream and egg until dough forms. Fold in pear and chopped walnuts.

3 On cookie sheet, pat dough into 8-inch round (if dough is sticky, dip fingers in Bisquick mix). Sprinkle with coarse sugar. Using sharp knife, cut round into 8 wedges, but do not separate. Place walnut half on top of each wedge.

4 Bake 12 to 15 minutes or until golden brown. Cool 5 minutes. Carefully separate wedges with knife; remove from cookie sheet to cooling rack. Serve warm.

*To toast walnuts, heat oven to 350°F. Bake walnuts in an ungreased pan about 10 minutes, stirring occasionally, until golden brown.

1 Scone: Calories 280; Total Fat 16g (Saturated Fat 5g; Trans Fat 0g); Cholesterol 0mg; Sodium 390mg; Total Carbohydrate 32g (Dietary Fiber 1g); Protein 5g **Exchanges:** 1½ Starch, 1½ Other Carbohydrate, 3 Fat **Carbohydrate Choices:** 2

Mediterranean Muffins

Prep Time: 20 Minutes • **Start to Finish:** 1 Hour • **12 muffins**

MUFFINS

2¼ cups Original Bisquick® mix

½ teaspoon dried dill weed

⅔ cup milk

1 egg

⅓ cup kalamata olives, pitted, chopped

⅓ cup crumbled feta cheese

¼ cup chopped drained roasted red bell peppers (from a jar)

¼ cup finely chopped green onions (4 medium)

1 tablespoon butter, melted

TOPPING

¾ cup chives-and-onion cream cheese spread, softened (from 8-oz container)

1 tablespoon milk

Sliced green onion, if desired

1 Heat oven to 350°F. Place foil baking cup in each of 12 regular-size muffin cups.

2 In large bowl, stir Bisquick mix, dill weed, ⅔ cup milk and the egg until soft dough forms. Gently fold in olives, feta cheese, roasted peppers and finely chopped green onions. Divide batter evenly among muffin cups; brush tops with melted butter.

3 Bake 16 to 18 minutes or until light golden brown. Cool 5 minutes. Remove muffins from pan to cooling rack. Cool 10 minutes.

4 Meanwhile, in small bowl, beat cream cheese spread and 1 tablespoon milk until smooth. Spread mixture over top of each muffin; sprinkle with sliced green onions.

1 Muffin: Calories 180; Total Fat 10g (Saturated Fat 4.5g; Trans Fat 1g); Cholesterol 35mg; Sodium 430mg; Total Carbohydrate 18g (Dietary Fiber 0g); Protein 4g **Exchanges:** 1 Other Carbohydrate, ½ Low-Fat Milk, 1½ Fat **Carbohydrate Choices:** 1

To pipe cream cheese topping onto muffins, place topping in a resealable food-storage plastic bag. Cut off small corner of bag; squeeze topping onto each muffin.

Parmesan-Chive Scones

Prep Time: 10 Minutes • **Start to Finish:** 25 Minutes • **6 scones**

2½ cups Bisquick Heart Smart® mix

1 cup shredded Parmesan cheese (4 oz)

¼ cup chopped fresh chives

1 egg

1 cup plain fat-free yogurt

1 Heat oven to 425°F. Lightly grease cookie sheet with shortening or cooking spray.

2 In large bowl, mix Bisquick mix, cheese and chives. In small bowl, beat egg and yogurt with fork or whisk until well blended; add to Bisquick mixture. Stir just until moistened.

3 Place dough on surface lightly sprinkled with Bisquick mix; gently roll in Bisquick mix to coat. Knead 4 to 5 times.

4 On cookie sheet, pat dough into 9-inch round. Using knife sprayed with cooking spray, cut round into 6 wedges, but do not separate.

5 Bake 11 to 12 minutes or until light golden brown. Carefully separate wedges with knife; remove from cookie sheet to cooling rack. Serve warm.

1 Scone: Calories 290; Total Fat 9g (Saturated Fat 3.5g; Trans Fat 0g); Cholesterol 45mg; Sodium 770mg; Total Carbohydrate 38g (Dietary Fiber 0g); Protein 13g **Exchanges:** 2 Starch, ½ Other Carbohydrate, 1 High-Fat Meat **Carbohydrate Choices:** 2½

Mini Beer–Pimiento Cheese Muffins

Prep Time: 10 Minutes • **Start to Finish:** 35 Minutes • 48 mini muffins

1 bottle (12 oz) beer, room temperature

1 jar (4 oz) diced pimientos, drained

1 egg

1 teaspoon finely grated onion

4 cups Original Bisquick® mix

2 cups shredded sharp Cheddar cheese (8 oz)

1 Heat oven to 400°F. Lightly spray 48 mini muffin cups with cooking spray.

2 In large bowl, mix beer, pimientos, egg and onion. Stir in Bisquick mix just until blended. (Batter may be lumpy.) Stir in cheese. Divide batter evenly among muffin cups.

3 Bake 13 to 15 minutes or until lightly browned. Remove muffins from pan to cooling rack. Cool 10 minutes. Serve warm.

1 Mini Muffin: Calories 65; Total Fat 3g (Saturated Fat 1g; Trans Fat 0g); Cholesterol 0mg; Sodium 156mg; Total Carbohydrate 7g (Dietary Fiber 0g); Protein 2g **Exchanges:** ½ Starch, ½ Fat **Carbohydrate Choices:** ½

These little muffins are a great snack or appetizer, or serve them alongside a bowl of soup or stew.

Mini Sour Cream–Butter Muffins

Prep Time: 10 Minutes • **Start to Finish:** 40 Minutes • **36 mini muffins**

2½ cups Original
  Bisquick® mix

¾ cup butter, melted

2 tablespoons chopped
  fresh chives

1 container (8 oz) sour
  cream

1 Heat oven to 350°F. Lightly spray 36 mini muffin cups with cooking spray.

2 In large bowl, mix all ingredients just until moistened. Divide batter evenly among muffin cups (cups will be almost full).

3 Bake 24 to 26 minutes or until light golden brown. Cool 2 minutes. Remove muffins from pan to cooling rack. Serve warm.

1 Mini Muffin: Calories 80; Total Fat 6g (Saturated Fat 4g; Trans Fat 0g); Cholesterol 0mg; Sodium 133mg; Total Carbohydrate 6g (Dietary Fiber 0g); Protein 1g **Exchanges:** ½ Starch, 1 Fat **Carbohydrate Choices:** ½

Try using basil or parsley instead of the chives.

Chicken and Green Chile Muffins

Prep Time: 15 Minutes • **Start to Finish:** 40 Minutes • 12 muffins

3 tablespoons butter

1 medium sweet onion, finely chopped (½ cup)

1½ cups Original Bisquick® mix

2 cups shredded Mexican cheese blend (8 oz)

1 egg

½ cup milk

1 cup finely chopped cooked chicken

1 can (4.5 oz) chopped green chiles

1 Heat oven to 425°F. Spray 12 regular-size muffin cups with cooking spray.

2 In 8-inch skillet, melt butter over medium heat. Add onion; cook 3 to 5 minutes, stirring frequently, until tender.

3 In large bowl, mix Bisquick mix and 1 cup of the cheese. In small bowl, stir egg and milk with fork or whisk until well blended; add to Bisquick mixture. Stir just until moistened. Stir in onion, chicken and chiles just until blended.

4 Divide batter evenly among muffin cups (⅔ full). Sprinkle remaining 1 cup cheese evenly over batter.

5 Bake 16 to 18 minutes or until golden brown. Cool 3 minutes. Remove muffins from pan to cooling rack. Serve warm.

1 Muffin: Calories 190; Total Fat 12g (Saturated Fat 6g; Trans Fat 0g); Cholesterol 0mg; Sodium 390mg; Total Carbohydrate 12g (Dietary Fiber 0g); Protein 10g **Exchanges:** 1 Starch, 1 Very Lean Meat, 2 Fat **Carbohydrate Choices:** 1

Berry Shortcake Muffins

Prep Time: 10 Minutes • **Start to Finish:** 30 Minutes • **12 muffins**

2 cups Original Bisquick® mix

⅓ cup sugar

⅔ cup whipping cream

2 tablespoons butter, melted

1 egg

¾ cup diced fresh strawberries

¾ cup fresh blueberries

Powdered sugar, if desired

1 Heat oven to 400°F. Place paper baking cup in each of 12 regular-size muffin cups; spray paper cups with cooking spray.

2 In large bowl, stir Bisquick mix, sugar, cream, butter and egg just until moistened. Fold in berries. Divide batter evenly among muffin cups.

3 Bake 15 to 16 minutes or until toothpick inserted in center comes out clean. Cool 5 minutes. Remove muffins from pan to cooling rack. Just before serving, sprinkle muffins with powdered sugar. Serve warm.

1 Muffin: Calories 190; Total Fat 8g (Saturated Fat 3.5g; Trans Fat 0g); Cholesterol 20mg; Sodium 310mg; Total Carbohydrate 26g (Dietary Fiber 0g); Protein 3g **Exchanges:** 1 Starch, ½ Other Carbohydrate, 1½ Fat **Carbohydrate Choices:** 2

Small blueberries will distribute between each muffin more evenly than large berries.

You can use frozen berries but do not thaw them before adding to the batter.

Impossibly Easy Raspberry–Cream Cheese Muffins

Prep Time: 20 Minutes • **Start to Finish:** 1 Hour • 12 muffins

MUFFINS

- 6 oz fresh raspberries
- 5 tablespoons granulated sugar
- 2 cups Original Bisquick® mix
- 3 tablespoons butter, melted
- 2 tablespoons cream cheese, softened
- ⅔ cup milk

TOPPING

- ½ cup Original Bisquick® mix
- ¼ cup packed brown sugar
- 3 tablespoons butter

GLAZE

- 1 tablespoon cream cheese, softened
- 1 tablespoon milk
- ½ cup powdered sugar

1 Heat oven to 375°F. Place paper baking cup in each of 12 regular-size muffin cups.

2 In small bowl, toss raspberries with 2 tablespoons of the granulated sugar; set aside.

3 In medium bowl, mix 2 cups Bisquick mix, the remaining 3 tablespoons granulated sugar, the melted butter, 2 tablespoons cream cheese and ⅔ cup milk until thick batter forms. Spoon 1 tablespoon batter into each muffin cup. Divide raspberries evenly over batter in muffin cups. Top with remaining batter; spread evenly.

4 In small bowl, mix ½ cup Bisquick mix and the brown sugar. Cut in 3 tablespoons butter, using pastry blender or fork, until mixture looks like crumbs. Sprinkle evenly over batter.

5 Bake 15 to 20 minutes or until golden brown. Cool 10 minutes. Remove muffins from pan to cooling rack.

6 Meanwhile, in small bowl, beat 1 tablespoon cream cheese and 1 tablespoon milk until smooth; stir in powdered sugar. Drizzle over tops of warm muffins.

1 Muffin: Calories 250; Total Fat 11g (Saturated Fat 5g; Trans Fat 1g); Cholesterol 20mg; Sodium 380mg; Total Carbohydrate 34g (Dietary Fiber 1g); Protein 2g **Exchanges:** ½ Starch, 2 Other Carbohydrate, 2 Fat **Carbohydrate Choices:** 2

Blueberry-Lime Muffins

Prep Time: 15 Minutes • **Start to Finish:** 40 Minutes • **12 muffins**

2 cups Original Bisquick® mix

½ cup packed brown sugar

1 teaspoon grated lime peel

¾ cup milk

¼ cup butter, melted

1 egg

1 cup fresh or frozen (do not thaw) blueberries

½ cup powdered sugar

1 tablespoon fresh lime juice

Additional grated lime peel, if desired

1 Heat oven to 400°F. Place paper baking cup in each of 12 regular-size muffin cups.

2 In large bowl, mix Bisquick mix, brown sugar and 1 teaspoon lime peel. In small bowl, stir milk, butter and egg with whisk or fork until well blended; add to Bisquick mixture. Stir just until moistened. Stir in blueberries. Divide batter evenly among muffin cups (¾ full).

3 Bake 16 to 18 minutes or until toothpick inserted in center comes out clean and tops are golden brown. Cool 5 minutes. Remove muffins from pan to cooling rack.

4 Meanwhile, in small bowl, mix powdered sugar and lime juice until well blended. Drizzle over muffins. Sprinkle with additional lime peel. Serve warm or at room temperature.

1 Muffin: Calories 200; Total Fat 7g (Saturated Fat 3.5g; Trans Fat 0g); Cholesterol 0mg; Sodium 300mg; Total Carbohydrate 31g (Dietary Fiber 0g); Protein 3g **Exchanges:** 1 Starch, 1 Other Carbohydrate, 1½ Fat **Carbohydrate Choices:** 2

Raspberry–White Chocolate Muffins

Prep Time: 10 Minutes • **Start to Finish:** 35 Minutes • 12 muffins

2 cups Original Bisquick® mix

½ cup white vanilla baking chips

⅓ cup sugar

⅔ cup milk

2 tablespoons vegetable oil

1 egg

1 cup raspberries

1 Heat oven to 400°F. Place paper baking cup in each of 12 regular-size muffin cups, or grease bottoms only with shortening or cooking spray.

2 In large bowl, stir all ingredients except raspberries just until moistened. Fold in raspberries. Divide batter evenly among muffin cups.

3 Bake 15 to 18 minutes or until golden brown. Cool 5 minutes. Remove muffins from pan to cooling rack. Serve warm.

1 Muffin: Calories 190; Total Fat 8g (Saturated Fat 3.5g; Trans Fat 0g); Cholesterol 20mg; Sodium 310mg; Total Carbohydrate 26g (Dietary Fiber 0g); Protein 3g **Exchanges:** 1 Starch, ½ Other Carbohydrate, 1½ Fat **Carbohydrate Choices:** 2

For a sweet finish, dip muffin tops into melted butter and then into coarse sugar crystals or granulated sugar. Or drizzle tops of muffins with melted white vanilla baking chips.

Pear and Ginger Muffins

Prep Time: 15 Minutes • **Start to Finish:** 35 Minutes • 12 muffins

2 cups Bisquick Heart
Smart® mix

⅔ cup milk

1 egg

⅓ cup packed brown sugar

2 tablespoons
vegetable oil

1 teaspoon
ground cinnamon

1 teaspoon
grated gingerroot

1 cup chopped unpeeled
pear

1 Heat oven to 400°F. Place paper baking cup in each of 12 regular-size muffin cups.

2 In medium bowl, mix all ingredients except pear. Fold in pear. Divide batter evenly among muffin cups.

3 Bake 17 to 20 minutes or until golden brown. Immediately remove muffins from pan to cooling rack. Serve warm or cool.

1 Muffin: Calories 140; Total Fat 4.5g (Saturated Fat 0.5g; Trans Fat 0g); Cholesterol 20mg; Sodium 180mg; Total Carbohydrate 22g (Dietary Fiber 0g); Protein 2g **Exchanges:** 1 Starch, ½ Other Carbohydrate, 1 Fat **Carbohydrate Choices:** 1½

Gingerroot can be found in the produce section at the grocery store. Peel it before grating. Wrap the unused portion tightly in foil and store it in the freezer.

Apple–Cinnamon Streusel Muffins

Prep Time: 15 Minutes • **Start to Finish:** 40 Minutes • 12 muffins

4 cups Original
   Bisquick® mix

¾ cup granulated sugar

3 teaspoons
   ground cinnamon

⅔ cup chunky applesauce

½ cup milk

¼ cup vegetable oil

2 eggs

3 tablespoons Original
   Bisquick® mix

¼ cup packed brown sugar

2 tablespoons butter,
   melted

1 Heat oven to 400°F. Spray 12 regular-size muffin cups with cooking spray.

2 In large bowl, mix 4 cups Bisquick mix, ½ cup of the granulated sugar and 2 teaspoons of the cinnamon. In small bowl, mix applesauce, milk, oil and eggs; add to Bisquick mixture. Stir just until moistened. Divide batter evenly among muffin cups (cups will be almost full).

3 In small bowl, mix 3 tablespoons Bisquick mix, remaining ¼ cup granulated sugar, remaining 1 teaspoon cinnamon and the brown sugar. Stir in butter until well blended. Sprinkle evenly over batter.

4 Bake 18 to 20 minutes or until toothpick inserted in center comes out clean and tops are golden brown. Cool 5 minutes. Remove muffins from pan to cooling rack. Serve warm.

1 Muffin: Calories 320; Total Fat 14g (Saturated Fat 4g; Trans Fat 0g); Cholesterol 0mg; Sodium 553mg; Total Carbohydrate 48g (Dietary Fiber 1g); Protein 5g **Exchanges:** 2 Starch, 1 Other Carbohydrate, 2½ Fat **Carbohydrate Choices:** 3

Orange Gingerbread Muffins

Prep Time: 10 Minutes • **Start to Finish:** 25 Minutes • **12 muffins**

2 cups Bisquick Heart Smart® mix

¼ cup cinnamon-sugar

½ teaspoon ground ginger

⅔ cup fat-free (skim) milk

¼ cup molasses

1 egg, slightly beaten

1 tablespoon grated orange peel

1 Heat oven to 400°F. Place paper baking cup in each of 12 regular-size muffin cups.

2 In large bowl, mix Bisquick mix, 3 tablespoons plus 1½ teaspoons of the cinnamon-sugar and the ginger. In small bowl, mix milk, molasses, egg and orange peel with whisk; add to Bisquick mixture. Stir just until moistened. Divide batter evenly among muffin cups (½ full). Sprinkle remaining 1½ teaspoons cinnamon-sugar over batter.

3 Bake 11 to 12 minutes. Immediately remove muffins from pan to cooling rack. Serve warm.

1 Muffin: Calories 116; Total Fat 2g (Saturated Fat 0g; Trans Fat 0g); Cholesterol 0mg; Sodium 234mg; Total Carbohydrate 23g (Dietary Fiber 1g); Protein 3g **Exchanges:** 1 Starch, ½ Other Carbohydrate **Carbohydrate Choices:** 1½

Peanut Butter–Chocolate Chip Muffins

Prep Time: 10 Minutes • **Start to Finish:** 35 Minutes • 18 muffins

2 cups Original Bisquick® mix

1 cup milk

½ cup sugar

2 eggs

½ cup chunky peanut butter

½ teaspoon vanilla

1 cup semisweet chocolate chips (6 oz)

1 Heat oven to 350°F. Place paper baking cup in each of 18 regular-size muffin cups; spray paper cups with cooking spray.

2 In large bowl, stir Bisquick mix, milk, sugar and eggs just until moistened. In small bowl, mix peanut butter and vanilla just until blended; stir in chocolate chips. Stir peanut butter mixture into batter. Divide batter evenly among muffin cups (⅔ full).

3 Bake 23 to 25 minutes or until light golden brown. Remove muffins from pan to cooling rack. Serve warm.

1 Muffin: Calories 195; Total Fat 10g (Saturated Fat 4g; Trans Fat 0g); Cholesterol 0mg; Sodium 214mg; Total Carbohydrate 25g (Dietary Fiber 1g); Protein 5g **Exchanges:** ½ Starch, 1 Other Carbohydrate, ½ Medium-Fat Meat, 1½ Fat **Carbohydrate Choices:** 1½

Easy Broccoli, Cheese and Ham Muffins

Prep Time: 15 Minutes • **Start to Finish:** 35 Minutes • 12 muffins

1 bag (12 oz) frozen broccoli and cheese sauce

1½ cups Original Bisquick® mix

½ cup milk

3 tablespoons vegetable oil

1 egg

½ cup diced cooked ham

½ cup shredded sharp Cheddar cheese (2 oz)

1 Heat oven to 400°F. Spray 12 regular-size muffin cups with cooking spray.

2 Cook broccoli as directed on bag.

3 In large bowl, stir Bisquick mix, milk, oil and egg just until moistened. Stir in broccoli, ham and cheese just until blended. Divide mixture evenly among muffin cups.

4 Bake 18 to 22 minutes or until golden brown. Cool 5 minutes. Remove muffins from pan to cooling rack. Serve warm.

1 Muffin: Calories 160; Total Fat 10g (Saturated Fat 3.5g; Trans Fat 0.5g); Cholesterol 30mg; Sodium 400mg; Total Carbohydrate 12g (Dietary Fiber 1g); Protein 6g **Exchanges:** 1 Starch, ½ Lean Meat, 1½ Fat **Carbohydrate Choices:** 1

> Wrap and refrigerate any leftover muffins. Unwrap and reheat one at a time on a microwavable plate for 15 to 30 seconds or until warm.

Mini Popovers with Flavored Butter Trio

Prep Time: 25 Minutes • **Start to Finish:** 50 Minutes • 32 mini popovers

POPOVER BATTER

¾ cup water

¼ cup butter

1 cup Original Bisquick® mix

4 eggs

APRICOT BUTTER, IF DESIRED

¼ cup butter, softened

2 tablespoons apricot preserves

HONEY-HERB BUTTER, IF DESIRED

¼ cup butter, softened

2 tablespoons chopped fresh parsley

1 teaspoon honey

MOLASSES BUTTER, IF DESIRED

¼ cup butter, softened

2 teaspoons mild molasses

1 Heat oven to 400°F. Generously grease 32 mini muffin cups with shortening.

2 In 4-quart saucepan, heat ¾ cup water and ¼ cup butter to rolling boil. Reduce heat to low; add Bisquick mix all at once. Stir vigorously with whisk about 1½ minutes or until mixture forms ball. Remove from heat. Beat in eggs, 1 at a time; continue beating until smooth.

3 Drop dough by level measuring tablespoonfuls into muffin cups.

4 Bake 23 to 27 minutes or until deep golden brown.

5 Meanwhile, stir together ingredients of desired flavored butter(s) to serve with popovers.

1 Mini Popover: Calories 40; Total Fat 2.5g (Saturated Fat 1.5g; Trans Fat 0g); Cholesterol 25mg; Sodium 65mg; Total Carbohydrate 3g (Dietary Fiber 0g); Protein 1g **Exchanges:** ½ Fat **Carbohydrate Choices:** 0

> The batter can be made and spooned into prepared mini muffin pans, covered and refrigerated up to 2 days in advance. Uncover and put directly in a preheated oven for fresh popovers in minutes!

Spicy Sweet Potato Biscuits

Prep Time: 10 Minutes • **Start to Finish:** 25 Minutes • 12 biscuits

2¾ cups Original Bisquick® mix

½ teaspoon ground red pepper (cayenne)

⅓ cup cold butter

1 cup mashed cooked sweet potatoes

½ cup milk

2 tablespoons butter, melted

Additional melted butter, if desired

1 Heat oven to 450°F. Spray cookie sheet with cooking spray.

2 In medium bowl, mix Bisquick mix and red pepper. Using pastry blender or fork, cut in ⅓ cup butter until mixture looks like coarse crumbs. In small bowl, mix sweet potatoes and milk until blended; add to crumb mixture. Stir with fork until dough leaves side of bowl.

3 Place dough on surface sprinkled with Bisquick mix; gently roll dough in Bisquick mix to coat. Knead lightly 6 to 8 times. Roll or pat dough to 1-inch thickness. With 2-inch round cutter dipped in Bisquick mix, cut dough into 12 rounds. Place about 1 inch apart on cookie sheet.

4 Bake 12 to 15 minutes or until light golden brown. Brush biscuits with melted butter. Serve immediately.

1 Biscuit: Calories 210; Total Fat 11g (Saturated Fat 6g; Trans Fat 1g); Cholesterol 20mg; Sodium 410mg; Total Carbohydrate 23g (Dietary Fiber 1g); Protein 3g **Exchanges:** 1 Starch, ½ Other Carbohydrate, 2 Fat **Carbohydrate Choices:** 1½

Tasty Biscuit Toppers

The aroma of fluffy, hot, homemade biscuits is all you need to call your crew to the table. Bisquick biscuits are a cinch to make—with just two ingredients. You can make drop biscuits by simply spooning the dough onto a cookie sheet, or roll and cut the dough, for a traditional biscuit shape.

BASIC BISCUITS

Start by mixing 2½ cups Original Bisquick® mix and ⅔ cup milk until a soft dough forms. **To make drop biscuits:** Drop the dough by 9 spoonfuls onto an ungreased cookie sheet. **To make rolled biscuits:** Place the dough on work surface well-sprinkled with Bisquick mix; knead 10 times. Roll dough to ½-inch thickness. Cut dough with 2½-inch cutter before placing on ungreased cookie sheet. **To bake:** Bake biscuits 8 to 10 minutes or until golden brown.

EASY TOPPING COMBOS

Although plain biscuits are wonderful, simply topped with butter or honey, it's nice to try something different on occasion. So take a break from the ordinary by topping your biscuits with one of these flavorful toppings before popping them in the oven. It's a quick and tasty way to up your dinner game!

Rosemary–Sea Salt Biscuits—Brush unbaked biscuits with 1 tablespoon melted butter or olive oil; sprinkle each lightly with ¼ teaspoon coarsely chopped fresh rosemary leaves and a dash of sea salt.

Bacon-Chive Biscuits—Mix 3 tablespoons finely chopped cooked bacon and 1 tablespoon finely chopped fresh chives in a small, shallow bowl. Dip the tops of unbaked biscuits into the bacon mixture, pressing lightly.

Garlic-Parmesan Biscuits—Brush unbaked biscuits with 1 tablespoon melted butter or olive oil. Mix 2 tablespoons grated Parmesan cheese and a dash of garlic powder; sprinkle over tops of biscuits.

Taco Biscuits—Mix 1 tablespoon melted butter or olive oil and ½ teaspoon taco seasoning in a small bowl; brush over unbaked biscuits.

Two-Seed Biscuits—Mix 2 tablespoons each sesame seed and poppy seed in a small, shallow bowl. Brush tops of unbaked biscuits with 1 tablespoon melted butter or olive oil. Dip the tops of biscuits into the seed mixture, pressing lightly.

Cheddar-Jalapeño Biscuits—Brush unbaked biscuits with 1 tablespoon melted butter or olive oil; sprinkle biscuits with ¼ cup finely shredded Cheddar cheese and about 2 teaspoons finely chopped green chiles (well drained) from a 4-ounce can.

Pesto-Romano Biscuits—Spread unbaked biscuits lightly with 1 tablespoon prepared pesto; sprinkle with 1 rounded tablespoon of grated Romano cheese.

Buffalo-Blue Biscuits—Spread unbaked biscuits lightly with 1 tablespoon prepared buffalo wing sauce; sprinkle with ¼ cup finely crumbled blue cheese; press lightly into biscuits.

Cheesy Bacon Pull-Apart Biscuits

Prep Time: 25 Minutes • **Start to Finish:** 50 Minutes • 8 biscuits

8 slices bacon

4½ cups Original Bisquick® mix

1⅓ cups milk

¼ cup chopped green onions (4 medium)

¼ teaspoon garlic powder

¼ teaspoon ground red pepper (cayenne)

1½ cups shredded sharp Cheddar cheese (6 oz)

¾ cup shredded mozzarella cheese (3 oz)

2 tablespoons chopped green onions (2 medium)

1 Heat oven to 400°F. In 9-inch cast-iron or other ovenproof skillet, cook bacon until crisp; drain on paper towels. Crumble bacon; set aside. Reserve 2 tablespoons drippings in skillet, coating bottom and side completely. Discard any remaining drippings.

2 In large bowl, stir Bisquick mix, milk, ¼ cup onions, the garlic powder and red pepper until soft dough forms.

3 Place dough on surface sprinkled with Bisquick mix; pat dough to 1-inch thickness. With 2½-inch round cutter, cut dough into 8 rounds. Arrange rounds in skillet; sprinkle ¾ cup of the Cheddar cheese evenly between rounds.

4 Bake 15 to 17 minutes or until light golden brown. Sprinkle mozzarella cheese and remaining ¾ cup Cheddar cheese on tops of biscuits. Bake 2 to 4 minutes longer or until cheese is melted. Sprinkle with bacon and 2 tablespoons onions. Serve warm.

1 Biscuit: Calories 367; Total Fat 19g (Saturated Fat 8g; Trans Fat 0g); Cholesterol 0mg; Sodium 1001mg; Total Carbohydrate 38g (Dietary Fiber 0g); Protein 13g **Exchanges:** 2½ Starch, 1 High-Fat Meat, 2 Fat **Carbohydrate Choices:** 2½

Cheddar Drop Biscuits

Prep Time: 10 Minutes • **Start to Finish:** 20 Minutes • 12 biscuits

2 cups Bisquick Heart Smart® mix

½ cup shredded reduced-fat sharp Cheddar cheese (2 oz)

¾ cup fat-free (skim) milk

2 tablespoons butter, melted

½ teaspoon parsley flakes, crushed

¼ teaspoon garlic powder

1 Heat oven to 450°F. Spray cookie sheet with cooking spray.

2 In medium bowl, mix Bisquick mix and cheese. Add milk, stir just until moistened.

3 Onto cookie sheet, drop dough by rounded tablespoonfuls about 2 inches apart.

4 Bake 8 to 10 minutes or until golden brown. In small bowl, mix butter, parsley flakes and garlic powder. Brush over warm biscuits; serve immediately.

1 Biscuit: Calories 110; Total Fat 4g (Saturated Fat 1g; Trans Fat 0g); Cholesterol 0mg; Sodium 284mg; Total Carbohydrate 15g (Dietary Fiber 1g); Protein 3g **Exchanges:** 1 Starch, 1 Fat **Carbohydrate Choices:** 1

Cheese-Garlic Biscuits

Prep Time: 10 Minutes • **Start to Finish:** 20 Minutes • 5 biscuits

1 cup Bisquick Heart Smart® mix

⅓ cup fat-free (skim) milk

¼ cup shredded reduced-fat Cheddar cheese (1 oz)

2 tablespoons butter, melted

⅛ teaspoon garlic powder

1 Heat oven to 450°F. In medium bowl, stir Bisquick mix, milk and cheese until soft dough forms.

2 Onto ungreased cookie sheet, drop dough by 5 spoonfuls.

3 Bake 8 to 10 minutes or until golden brown. In small bowl, mix butter and garlic powder; brush over warm biscuits. Serve warm.

1 Biscuit: Calories 140; Total Fat 7g (Saturated Fat 3g; Trans Fat 0g); Cholesterol 15mg; Sodium 350mg; Total Carbohydrate 17g (Dietary Fiber 0g); Protein 4g **Exchanges:** 1 Starch, 1½ Fat **Carbohydrate Choices:** 1

Mile-High Raspberry Coffee Cake

Prep Time: 20 Minutes • **Start to Finish:** 3 Hours • 10 servings

TOPPING

⅔ cup sliced almonds

½ cup all-purpose flour

⅓ cup sugar

3 tablespoons butter, melted

COFFEE CAKE

3 cups Original Bisquick® mix

1 cup sugar

1 cup vanilla low-fat yogurt

½ cup almond meal

¼ cup butter, melted

¼ cup milk

2 teaspoons vanilla

2 eggs

2 cups frozen raspberries (do not thaw)

1 tablespoon all-purpose flour

1 Heat oven to 325°F. Generously spray 9-inch springform pan with cooking spray.

2 In medium bowl, mix almonds, ½ cup flour and ⅓ cup sugar. Gradually stir in 3 tablespoons melted butter until blended. Use fingers to pinch topping into clumps.

3 In large bowl, beat Bisquick mix, 1 cup sugar, the yogurt, almond meal, ¼ cup melted butter, the milk, vanilla and eggs with spoon until well blended. Spread batter in pan. In small bowl, toss raspberries with 1 tablespoon flour; sprinkle over batter. Sprinkle with topping.

4 Bake 1 hour to 1 hour 10 minutes or until toothpick inserted in center comes out clean. Cool completely on cooling rack, about 1 hour 30 minutes. Run thin knife around side of cake; remove side of pan.

1 Serving: Calories 500; Total Fat 21g (Saturated Fat 8g; Trans Fat 1g); Cholesterol 60mg; Sodium 540mg; Total Carbohydrate 69g (Dietary Fiber 5g); Protein 8g **Exchanges:** 2½ Starch, 2 Other Carbohydrate, 4 Fat **Carbohydrate Choices:** 4½

Banana-Toffee Coffee Cakes

Prep Time: 20 Minutes • **Start to Finish:** 50 Minutes • 12 coffee cakes

COFFEE CAKES

- 2 cups Original Bisquick® mix
- ⅓ cup granulated sugar
- 1 cup mashed very ripe bananas (2 medium)
- ⅔ cup milk
- 1 egg, slightly beaten
- ½ teaspoon ground allspice

TOPPING

- ½ cup all-purpose flour
- ½ cup packed brown sugar
- ¼ cup cold butter
- 2 tablespoons peanut butter

GLAZE

- ½ cup white vanilla baking chips
- 2 tablespoons whipping cream

1 Heat oven to 400°F. Spray 12 regular-size muffin cups with cooking spray.

2 In medium bowl, stir coffee cake ingredients with fork or whisk until blended. Divide batter evenly among muffin cups.

3 In small bowl, mix flour and brown sugar. Cut in butter and peanut butter, using pastry blender or fork, until mixture looks like small peas. Sprinkle topping evenly over batter in cups.

4 Bake 16 to 18 minutes or until toothpick inserted in center comes out clean. Cool 10 minutes. Remove coffee cakes from pan to cooling rack.

5 In small microwavable bowl, microwave baking chips and whipping cream uncovered on High 30 to 60 seconds or until chips are melted; stir until smooth. Place sheet of waxed paper under cooling rack. Drizzle glaze back and forth over tops of coffee cakes with tines of fork. Serve warm.

1 Coffee Cake: Calories 300; Total Fat 12g (Saturated Fat 7g; Trans Fat 1g); Cholesterol 30mg; Sodium 310mg; Total Carbohydrate 43g (Dietary Fiber 1g); Protein 4g **Exchanges:** 1½ Starch, 1½ Other Carbohydrate, 2 Fat **Carbohydrate Choices:** 3

Gluten-Free Fruit Swirl Coffee Cake

Prep Time: 20 Minutes • **Start to Finish:** 45 Minutes • 18 servings

COFFEE CAKE

- 4 **eggs**
- ¾ **cup milk**
- ½ **cup butter, melted**
- 2 **teaspoons gluten-free vanilla**
- 1 **box Bisquick® Gluten Free mix (3 cups)**
- ⅔ **cup granulated sugar**
- 1 **can (21 oz) gluten-free fruit pie filling (any flavor)**

GLAZE

- 1 **cup powdered sugar**
- 2 **tablespoons milk**

1 Heat oven to 375°F. Grease a 15x10x1-inch pan or 2 (9-inch) square pans with shortening or cooking spray (without flour).

2 In large bowl, stir all coffee cake ingredients except pie filling until blended; beat vigorously 30 seconds. Spread two-thirds of the batter (about 2½ cups) in 15x10x1-inch pan or one-third of the batter (about 1¼ cups) in each square pan.

3 Spread pie filling over batter (filling may not cover batter completely). Drop remaining batter by tablespoonfuls onto pie filling.

4 Bake 20 to 25 minutes or until golden brown. Meanwhile, in small bowl, mix glaze ingredients until smooth. Drizzle glaze over warm coffee cake. Serve warm or cool.

1 Serving: Calories 240; Total Fat 7g (Saturated Fat 4g; Trans Fat 0g); Cholesterol 60mg; Sodium 280mg; Total Carbohydrate 41g (Dietary Fiber 0g); Protein 3g **Exchanges:** 1 Starch, 1½ Other Carbohydrate, 1½ Fat **Carbohydrate Choices:** 3

If you are cooking gluten free, always read labels to make sure each recipe ingredient is gluten free. Products and ingredient sources can change.

This easy fruit-filled coffee cake is ripe for any flavor of filling—take your pick! Try apple, cherry, blueberry, peach or apricot pie filling. Or try gluten-free lemon curd for a luscious citrus twist.

Sweet Potato–Caramel Twist Coffee Cake

Prep Time: 25 Minutes • **Start to Finish:** 55 Minutes • **12 servings**

⅓ cup butter

½ cup packed brown sugar

¼ cup corn syrup

½ cup chopped pecans

2½ cups Original Bisquick® mix

⅔ cup mashed canned vacuum-pack sweet potatoes

⅓ cup milk

2 tablespoons butter, softened

3 tablespoons packed brown sugar

1 Heat oven to 400°F. In ungreased 9-inch square pan, melt ⅓ cup butter in oven. Stir in ½ cup brown sugar and the corn syrup. Sprinkle with pecans.

2 In medium bowl, stir Bisquick mix, sweet potatoes and milk until dough forms a ball.

3 Place dough on surface sprinkled with Bisquick mix; gently roll in Bisquick mix to coat. Lightly knead 10 times. Roll or pat dough into 12-inch square. Spread 2 tablespoons butter over dough. Sprinkle 3 tablespoons brown sugar over butter. Fold dough into thirds; press edges together to seal. Cut crosswise into 12 (1-inch) strips. Twist ends of each strip in opposite directions. Arrange twists on pecans in pan.

4 Bake 25 to 30 minutes or until golden brown. Immediately place heatproof serving plate upside down onto pan; carefully turn plate and pan over. Leave pan over coffee cake 1 minute; remove pan. Serve warm.

1 Serving: Calories 290; Total Fat 14g (Saturated Fat 6g; Trans Fat 1g); Cholesterol 20mg; Sodium 390mg; Total Carbohydrate 38g (Dietary Fiber 1g); Protein 3g **Exchanges:** 1 Starch, 1½ Other Carbohydrate, 2½ Fat **Carbohydrate Choices:** 2½

> **Serve this scrumptious coffee cake with fresh fruit and orange juice.**

Glazed Sweetheart Rolls

Prep Time: 20 Minutes • **Start to Finish:** 35 Minutes • 24 rolls

ROLLS

4½ cups Original Bisquick® mix

1⅓ cups milk

¼ teaspoon almond extract

2 tablespoons butter, softened

1 box (4-serving size) raspberry- or strawberry-flavored gelatin (not sugar free)

FROSTING

2 cups powdered sugar

2 to 3 tablespoons milk or water

1 teaspoon vanilla

1 Heat oven to 425°F. Grease cookie sheet with shortening or cooking spray.

2 In large bowl, stir Bisquick mix, 1⅓ cups milk and the almond extract until soft dough forms.

3 Place dough on surface generously sprinkled with Bisquick mix; gently roll in Bisquick mix to coat. Shape dough into ball; knead 10 times.

4 Divide dough in half. Roll or pat each half into 12x7-inch rectangle. Spread 1 tablespoon of the butter over each rectangle. Sprinkle half of the gelatin over each rectangle; spread evenly with back of spoon. Roll up each rectangle tightly, beginning at 12-inch side; pinch edge of dough into roll to seal. Cut each roll into 12 (1-inch) slices. Place on cookie sheet 1 inch apart.

5 To make heart shape, pinch one side of each slice to form sharp point; make deep indentation in opposite side of slice with knife to make top of heart.

6 Bake 12 to 15 minutes or until golden brown.

7 Meanwhile, in medium bowl, mix frosting ingredients until smooth and spreadable. Remove rolls from cookie sheet to cooling rack; spread icing over warm rolls.

1 Roll: Calories 160; Total Fat 4g (Saturated Fat 1.5g; Trans Fat 1g); Cholesterol 0mg; Sodium 310mg; Total Carbohydrate 29g (Dietary Fiber 0g); Protein 2g **Exchanges:** 1 Starch, 1 Other Carbohydrate, ½ Fat **Carbohydrate Choices:** 2

To save time, skip the heart shape and make regular round rolls.

Hurry-Up Homemade Crescent Rolls

Prep Time: 25 Minutes • **Start to Finish:** 1 Hour 45 Minutes • 12 rolls

1 package regular active dry yeast (2¼ teaspoons)

¾ cup warm water (105°F to 115°F)

3 to 3½ cups Original Bisquick® mix

2 tablespoons sugar

Poppy seed, if desired

1 In small bowl, mix yeast and warm water; let stand 5 minutes. In large bowl, mix 3 cups of the Bisquick mix and the sugar; gradually stir in yeast mixture until dough forms.

2 Place dough on surface sprinkled with Bisquick mix; gently roll in Bisquick to coat. Knead 10 minutes or until dough is smooth and elastic, adding remaining ½ cup Bisquick mix as needed.

3 Roll dough into 12-inch round; cut into 12 wedges. Roll up wedges, starting at wide end, to form crescent shape. Spray cookie sheet with cooking spray. Place rolls, point side down, 2 inches apart on cookie sheet. Cover loosely with plastic wrap and cloth towel. Let rise in warm place (80°F to 85°F) 1 hour or until doubled in size.

4 Heat oven to 425°F. Uncover rolls. Sprinkle with poppy seed, if you like. Bake 10 to 12 minutes or until golden. Serve warm.

1 Roll: Calories 141; Total Fat 5g (Saturated Fat 1g; Trans Fat 0g); Cholesterol 0mg; Sodium 402mg; Total Carbohydrate 24g (Dietary Fiber 0g); Protein 3g **Exchanges:** 1 Starch, ½ Other Carbohydrate, 1 Fat **Carbohydrate Choices:** 1½

Banana Nut Bread

Prep Time: 15 Minutes • **Start to Finish:** 3 Hours 25 Minutes • 1 loaf (24 slices)

1⅓ cups mashed very ripe bananas (2 large)

⅔ cup sugar

¼ cup milk

3 tablespoons vegetable oil

½ teaspoon vanilla

3 eggs

2⅔ cups Original Bisquick® mix

½ cup chopped nuts

1 Heat oven to 350°F. Grease bottom only of 9x5-inch loaf pan with shortening.

2 In large bowl, mix bananas, sugar, milk, oil, vanilla and eggs. Stir in Bisquick mix and nuts. Pour batter into pan.

3 Bake 50 to 60 minutes or until toothpick inserted in center comes out clean. Cool 10 minutes. Run knife or metal spatula around sides of pan to loosen bread; remove from pan to cooling rack. Cool completely, about 2 hours.

1 Slice: Calories 130; Total Fat 6g (Saturated Fat 1g; Trans Fat 0g); Cholesterol 25mg; Sodium 170mg; Total Carbohydrate 18g (Dietary Fiber 0g); Protein 2g **Exchanges:** ½ Starch, ½ Other Carbohydrate, 1 Vegetable, 1 Fat **Carbohydrate Choices:** 1

This bread freezes well and is great to have on hand when company drops in. Freeze by wrapping it tightly in heavy-duty foil for up to 2 months. To store, wrap bread tightly in plastic wrap or foil. Store at room temperature up to 4 days, or refrigerate up to 10 days.

Make terrific banana bread French toast. Dip bread in egg mixture, and cook in skillet 2 to 3 minutes on each side or until golden brown. It's delicious topped with maple syrup.

Blueberry-Banana-Oat Bread

Prep Time: 10 Minutes • **Start to Finish:** 3 Hours 15 Minutes • 1 loaf (24 slices)

2¼ cups Original Bisquick® mix

⅔ cup sugar

⅓ cup quick-cooking oats

1 cup mashed very ripe bananas (2 medium)

¼ cup milk

2 eggs

1 cup fresh or frozen (thawed and drained) blueberries

1 Heat oven to 350°F. Grease bottom only of 9x5-inch loaf pan with shortening.

2 In large bowl, stir Bisquick mix, sugar, oats, bananas, milk and eggs until moistened; beat vigorously 30 seconds. Gently stir in blueberries. Pour batter into pan.

3 Bake 50 to 55 minutes or until toothpick inserted in center comes out clean. Cool 10 minutes. Run knife or metal spatula around sides of pan to loosen bread; remove from pan to cooling rack. Cool completely, about 2 hours.

1 Slice: Calories 90; Total Fat 2g (Saturated Fat 0.5g; Trans Fat 0g); Cholesterol 20mg; Sodium 170mg; Total Carbohydrate 16g (Dietary Fiber 0g); Protein 2g **Exchanges:** 1 Starch **Carbohydrate Choices:** 1

Cranberry Bread

Prep Time: 20 Minutes • **Start to Finish:** 3 Hours 30 Minutes • 1 loaf (24 slices)

2⅓ cups Bisquick Heart Smart® mix

¾ cup granulated sugar

½ cup reduced-fat sour cream

¼ cup vegetable oil

¼ cup fat-free (skim) milk

2 tablespoons grated orange peel (from 2 oranges)

5 egg whites or ¾ cup fat-free egg product

¾ cup fresh or frozen cranberries, chopped

½ cup powdered sugar

2 to 3 teaspoons orange juice

1 Heat oven to 375°F. Generously grease bottom only of 9x5-inch loaf pan. In medium bowl, stir Bisquick mix, granulated sugar, sour cream, oil, milk, orange peel and egg whites until moistened. Stir in cranberries. Pour batter into pan.

2 Bake 50 to 55 minutes or until toothpick inserted in center comes out clean and top crust is deep golden brown. Cool 15 minutes. Run knife or metal spatula around sides of pan to loosen bread; remove from pan to cooling rack. Cool completely, about 2 hours.

3 In small bowl, stir powdered sugar and orange juice until smooth and thin enough to drizzle. Drizzle over bread.

1 Slice: Calories 110; Total Fat 3.5g (Saturated Fat 0.5g; Trans Fat 0g); Cholesterol 0mg; Sodium 115mg; Total Carbohydrate 18g (Dietary Fiber 0g); Protein 2g **Exchanges:** 1 Starch, ½ Fat **Carbohydrate Choices:** 1

Freeze this tasty quick bread by wrapping it tightly in heavy-duty foil for up to 2 months. To store, wrap bread tightly in plastic wrap or foil. Store at room temperature up to 4 days, or refrigerate up to 10 days.

When grating orange peel, be sure to grate only the orange part of the skin. The white part, or pith, is very bitter.

Maple Walnut Bread

Prep Time: 10 Minutes • **Start to Finish:** 2 Hours 25 Minutes • 1 loaf (12 slices)

2 teaspoons shortening

1 teaspoon all-purpose flour

2 cups Original Bisquick® mix

⅔ cup sugar

½ cup quick-cooking oats

⅓ cup chopped walnuts, toasted*

½ cup vegetable oil

½ cup sour cream

⅓ cup real maple syrup

¼ cup milk

2 eggs

1 Heat oven to 350°F. Grease bottom and sides of 9x5-inch loaf pan with shortening; lightly flour.

2 In large bowl, mix Bisquick mix, sugar, oats and walnuts. Stir in remaining ingredients until blended. Pour batter into pan.

3 Bake 1 hour to 1 hour 5 minutes or until toothpick inserted in center comes out clean and bread is firm to the touch. Cool 10 minutes. Run knife or metal spatula around sides of pan to loosen bread; remove from pan to cooling rack. Cool completely, about 1 hour.

*To toast walnuts, heat oven to 350°F. Bake walnuts in an ungreased pan about 10 minutes, stirring occasionally, until golden brown.

1 Slice: Calories 300; Total Fat 18g (Saturated Fat 3.5g; Trans Fat 0g); Cholesterol 0mg; Sodium 270mg; Total Carbohydrate 34g (Dietary Fiber 1g); Protein 4g **Exchanges:** 1 Starch, 1 Other Carbohydrate, 3½ Fat **Carbohydrate Choices:** 2

Spinach-Cheese Bread

Prep Time: 20 Minutes • **Start to Finish:** 1 Hour 45 Minutes • 1 loaf (16 slices)

3 cups Original Bisquick® mix

¼ cup vegetable oil

1 tablespoon caraway seed

3 eggs

1 can (10.75 oz) condensed Cheddar cheese soup

1 box (9 oz) frozen chopped spinach, thawed, squeezed to drain*

1 Heat oven to 350°F. Grease bottom and sides of 9x5-inch loaf pan with shortening.

2 In large bowl, stir all ingredients except spinach until blended; beat with spoon 1 minute. Stir in spinach. Pour batter into pan.

3 Bake 55 to 65 minutes or until toothpick inserted in center comes out clean. Cool 20 minutes. Run knife or metal spatula around sides of pan to loosen bread; remove from pan to cooling rack. Serve warm, or cool completely.

*To quickly thaw spinach, cut a small slit in the center of the pouch. Microwave on High 2 to 3 minutes or until thawed. Remove spinach from the pouch and squeeze dry with paper towels.

1 Slice: Calories 160; Total Fat 9g (Saturated Fat 2.5g; Trans Fat 1g); Cholesterol 45mg; Sodium 470mg; Total Carbohydrate 17g (Dietary Fiber 1g); Protein 4g **Exchanges:** 1 Starch, 2 Fat **Carbohydrate Choices:** 1

You can use 1 tablespoon dried minced onion in place of the caraway seed.

Pizza Bread

Prep Time: 10 Minutes • **Start to Finish:** 3 Hours 10 Minutes • 1 loaf (16 slices)

3¾ cups Bisquick Heart Smart® mix

1 cup shredded reduced-fat mozzarella cheese (4 oz)

1 teaspoon Italian seasoning

15 slices turkey pepperoni, cut into quarters

1½ cups 1% low-fat milk

¼ cup fat-free egg product

2 tablespoons butter, melted

⅓ cup sun-dried tomato pesto

1 Heat oven to 350°F. Spray 9x5-inch loaf pan with cooking spray.

2 In large bowl, mix Bisquick mix, cheese, Italian seasoning and pepperoni. Add milk, egg product and melted butter; stir just until moistened. Add pesto; gently swirl into batter (do not completely combine). Spoon batter into pan.

3 Bake 50 to 55 minutes or until toothpick inserted in center comes out clean. Cool 5 minutes. Run knife or metal spatula around sides of pan to loosen bread; remove from pan to cooling rack. Cool completely, about 2 hours.

1 Slice: Calories 230; Total Fat 9g (Saturated Fat 3g; Trans Fat 0g); Cholesterol 0mg; Sodium 940mg; Total Carbohydrate 22g (Dietary Fiber 0g); Protein 14g **Exchanges:** 1½ Starch, 1 Lean Meat, ½ Medium-Fat Meat, 1 Fat **Carbohydrate Choices:** 1½

CHAPTER 3

Get Ready for Breakfast

Pear-Topped Buttermilk Pancakes

Prep Time: 30 Minutes • **Start to Finish:** 30 Minutes • 14 servings

TOPPING

4	ripe pears, peeled, sliced
1	tablespoon fresh lemon juice
1	tablespoon honey
¼	teaspoon ground cinnamon
1½	teaspoons butter

PANCAKES

2	cups Bisquick Heart Smart® mix
2	cups fat-free buttermilk
1	egg

1 In medium bowl, toss pears, lemon juice, honey and cinnamon. In 12-inch nonstick skillet, melt butter over medium-high heat. Add pear mixture; cook 8 to 10 minutes, stirring occasionally, until slightly thickened. Remove from heat; cover to keep warm.

2 In another medium bowl, stir Bisquick mix, buttermilk and egg with fork or whisk until blended.

3 Heat griddle or skillet over medium-high heat (375°F). Brush griddle with vegetable oil if necessary (or spray with cooking spray before heating).

4 For each pancake, pour ¼ cup batter onto hot griddle. Cook until bubbles form on top and edges are dry. Turn; cook other side until golden brown.

5 Serve pancakes with warm pear topping.

1 Serving: Calories 116; Total Fat 2g (Saturated Fat 0g; Trans Fat 0g); Cholesterol 0mg; Sodium 229mg; Total Carbohydrate 23g (Dietary Fiber 2g); Protein 3g **Exchanges:** 1½ Starch **Carbohydrate Choices:** 1½

Pumpkin Waffles with Maple-Apple Syrup

Prep Time: 20 Minutes • **Start to Finish:** 20 Minutes • 6 servings (2 waffles and 2 tablespoons syrup each)

SYRUP

½ cup maple-flavored syrup

¼ cup frozen (thawed) apple juice concentrate

WAFFLES

2⅓ cups Original Bisquick® mix

1½ cups milk

½ cup canned pumpkin (not pumpkin pie mix)

¼ cup vegetable oil

2 tablespoons packed brown sugar

1 teaspoon pumpkin pie spice

2 eggs

¼ cup chopped pecans

Powdered sugar, if desired

1 In 1-quart saucepan, heat syrup ingredients, stirring occasionally, until juice concentrate is melted and mixture is warm.

2 Heat waffle maker. (Waffle makers without a nonstick coating may need to be brushed with vegetable oil or sprayed with cooking spray before batter for each waffle is added.)

3 In large bowl, beat all waffle ingredients except pecans and powdered sugar with whisk or hand beater until blended.

4 For each waffle, pour batter onto center of hot waffle maker. (Waffle makers vary in size; check manufacturer's directions for recommended amount of batter.) Close lid of waffle maker.

5 Bake about 5 minutes or until steaming stops and waffle is golden brown. Carefully remove waffle. Serve immediately with syrup; top with pecans and powdered sugar. Repeat with remaining batter.

1 Serving: Calories 480; Total Fat 22g (Saturated Fat 4.5g; Trans Fat 1g); Cholesterol 75mg; Sodium 740mg; Total Carbohydrate 64g (Dietary Fiber 2g); Protein 8g **Exchanges:** 2 Starch, 2½ Other Carbohydrate, 4 Fat **Carbohydrate Choices:** 4

In place of the pumpkin pie spice, use ¼ teaspoon each of ground cinnamon, ground nutmeg and ground ginger instead.

Apple Oven Pancake

Prep Time: 25 Minutes • **Start to Finish:** 55 Minutes • **8 servings**

3 tablespoons butter

4 medium cooking apples, peeled, thinly sliced (about 6 cups)

¼ cup packed brown sugar

2 teaspoons ground cinnamon

1½ cups Original Bisquick® mix

¼ cup granulated sugar

1 cup buttermilk

1 tablespoon fresh lemon juice

1 teaspoon vanilla

2 eggs

1 tablespoon cinnamon-sugar

Maple-flavored syrup, if desired

1 Heat oven to 450°F. In oven, melt butter in 10-inch ovenproof or cast-iron skillet, about 2 minutes. Add apples, brown sugar and cinnamon; toss to coat apples. (Pan will be very hot.) Bake 2 minutes longer; stir. Bake 3 minutes longer; stir again. Reduce oven temperature to 400°F.

2 In large bowl, beat Bisquick mix, granulated sugar, buttermilk, lemon juice, vanilla and eggs with whisk or fork until blended. Pour over apples.

3 Bake 25 to 30 minutes or until golden brown. Sprinkle with cinnamon-sugar. Cut into wedges. Drizzle with syrup. Serve immediately.

1 Serving: Calories 280; Total Fat 9g (Saturated Fat 4.5g, Trans Fat 1g); Cholesterol 65mg; Sodium 370mg; Total Carbohydrate 43g (Dietary Fiber 2g); Protein 5g **Exchanges:** 1 Starch, ½ Fruit, 1½ Other Carbohydrate, 1½ Fat **Carbohydrate Choices:** 3

The best baking apples are slightly tart and top choices are Braeburn, Granny Smith, Cortland, Northern Spy and Rome Beauty.

Make weekend mornings special and breakfast a little heartier by serving this oven pancake with sausage or bacon.

Blueberry-Orange Pancakes

Prep Time: 30 Minutes • **Start to Finish:** 30 Minutes • 7 servings (2 pancakes and about 3 tablespoons sauce each)

SAUCE

- ¼ **cup sugar**
- 1½ **teaspoons cornstarch**
- ¼ **teaspoon grated orange peel**
- 2 **tablespoons orange juice**
- 2 **cups fresh or frozen unsweetened blueberries**

PANCAKES

- 2 **cups Original Bisquick® mix**
- 1 **cup milk**
- 1 **teaspoon grated orange peel**
- ¼ **teaspoon ground nutmeg**
- 2 **eggs**
- 1 **cup fresh or frozen unsweetened blueberries (do not thaw)**

1 In 1½-quart saucepan, mix sugar, cornstarch, ¼ teaspoon orange peel and the orange juice until smooth. Stir in 2 cups blueberries. Heat to boiling over medium heat, stirring constantly. Boil about 2 minutes, stirring occasionally, until thickened. Keep warm.

2 In medium bowl, stir all pancake ingredients except blueberries until blended. Gently stir in 1 cup blueberries.

3 Heat griddle or 12-inch skillet over medium-high heat (375°F). Brush griddle with vegetable oil if necessary (or spray with cooking spray before heating).

4 For each pancake, pour slightly less than ¼ cup batter onto hot griddle. Cook until edges are dry. Turn; cook other side until golden brown. Serve with warm sauce.

1 Serving: Calories 250; Total Fat 7g (Saturated Fat 2g; Trans Fat 1g); Cholesterol 65mg; Sodium 520mg; Total Carbohydrate 40g (Dietary Fiber 2g); Protein 6g **Exchanges:** 2 Starch, ½ Fruit, 1½ Fat **Carbohydrate Choices:** 2½

Blueberries are great to have on hand in the freezer. When using the frozen blueberries in pancakes, be sure to blot them with paper towels to keep the juice from staining the batter.

Gluten-Free Blueberry–Sour Cream Pancakes

Prep Time: 20 Minutes • **Start to Finish:** 20 Minutes • 4 servings (3 pancakes each)

1 cup Bisquick® Gluten Free mix

1 cup milk

2 tablespoons vegetable oil

1 egg

¼ cup sour cream

1 cup fresh or frozen blueberries (do not thaw)

Butter, if desired

Maple syrup, if desired

1 In large bowl, stir Bisquick mix, milk, oil and egg until well blended. Stir in sour cream; gently stir in blueberries.

2 Heat griddle or skillet over medium-high heat (375°F). Brush griddle with vegetable oil if necessary (or spray with cooking spray without flour before heating).

3 For each pancake, pour ¼ cup batter onto hot griddle. Cook until edges are dry. Turn; cook other side until golden brown. Serve with butter and maple syrup.

1 Serving: Calories 270; Total Fat 13g (Saturated Fat 4g; Trans Fat 0g); Cholesterol 65mg; Sodium 390mg; Total Carbohydrate 34g (Dietary Fiber 1g); Protein 5g **Exchanges:** 1 Starch, ½ Fruit, ½ Other Carbohydrate, 2½ Fat **Carbohydrate Choices:** 2

> If you are cooking gluten free, always read labels to make sure each recipe ingredient is gluten free. Products and ingredient sources can change.

Vanilla Pancakes with Quinoa and Blueberries

Prep Time: 35 Minutes • **Start to Finish:** 35 Minutes • 8 servings (2 pancakes each)

PANCAKES

- ½ cup old-fashioned oats
- ⅔ cup fat-free (skim) milk
- 1½ cups Greek fat-free vanilla yogurt
- 2 eggs
- 2 cups Bisquick Heart Smart® mix
- ½ cup chopped walnuts
- ¼ cup ground flaxseed or flaxseed meal
- ½ cup cooked quinoa
- 1 teaspoon baking soda
- 1 cup fresh or frozen blueberries (do not thaw)

TOPPINGS, IF DESIRED

- Real maple syrup
- Additional Greek fat-free vanilla yogurt
- Additional blueberries
- Additional chopped walnuts

1 In large bowl, place oats; add milk; stir. Let stand 5 minutes.

2 Add yogurt and eggs to oatmeal mixture; mix well. Add remaining pancake ingredients except blueberries; stir until blended. (Batter will be thick.)

3 Heat nonstick griddle or skillet over medium-low heat (350°F). Brush griddle with vegetable oil if necessary (or spray with cooking spray before heating).

4 For each pancake, pour about ¼ cup batter onto griddle; spread to 4 inches in diameter. Sprinkle 1 tablespoon blueberries over each pancake. Cook about 2 minutes on each side or until golden brown and cooked through.

5 Serve with toppings.

1 Serving: Calories 280; Total Fat 10g (Saturated Fat 1g; Trans Fat 0g); Cholesterol 50mg; Sodium 460mg; Total Carbohydrate 36g (Dietary Fiber 2g); Protein 12g **Exchanges:** 2 Starch, ½ Other Carbohydrate, 1 Very Lean Meat, 1½ Fat **Carbohydrate Choices:** 2½

> Freeze these pancakes for a quick weekday breakfast. Cool pancakes completely on a cooling rack. Place in a resealable freezer plastic bag or container. To reheat, microwave one frozen pancake uncovered on a microwavable plate on High 20 to 30 seconds or three pancakes at a time, about 1 minute. Or, pop a pancake in the toaster to reheat.
>
> Next time you are making quinoa, make a little extra to save for this recipe.

Walnut Pancakes with Marmalade

Prep Time: 25 Minutes • **Start to Finish:** 25 Minutes • 8 servings (2 pancakes and about 2 tablespoons marmalade mixture each)

1 cup orange marmalade

½ cup sweetened dried cranberries or dried cherries

2 tablespoons water

½ teaspoon vanilla

2½ cups Original Bisquick® mix

1 cup milk

1 tablespoon sugar

½ teaspoon grated lemon peel

2 tablespoons fresh lemon juice

2 teaspoons baking powder

2 eggs

1 cup chopped walnuts, toasted*

Additional toasted chopped walnuts, if desired

1 In small microwavable bowl, microwave marmalade uncovered on High 30 to 60 seconds, stirring occasionally, until melted and smooth. Stir in cranberries, water and vanilla. Microwave on High 20 to 30 seconds or until thoroughly heated. Cover to keep warm.

2 In large bowl, stir Bisquick mix, milk, sugar, lemon peel, lemon juice, baking powder and eggs with fork or whisk until blended. Stir in 1 cup walnuts.

3 Heat griddle or skillet over medium-high heat (375°F). Brush griddle with vegetable oil if necessary (or spray with cooking spray before heating).

4 For each pancake, pour ¼ cup batter onto hot griddle. Cook 2 to 3 minutes or until bubbles form on top and edges are dry. Turn; cook other side until golden brown.

5 Serve pancakes with marmalade mixture and additional walnuts.

*To toast walnuts, heat oven to 350°F. Bake walnuts in an ungreased pan about 10 minutes, stirring occasionally, until golden brown.

1 Serving: Calories 414; Total Fat 16g (Saturated Fat 3g; Trans Fat 0g); Cholesterol 0mg; Sodium 656mg; Total Carbohydrate 64g (Dietary Fiber 3g); Protein 8g **Exchanges:** 1½ Starch, ½ Fruit, 2 Other Carbohydrate, ½ Medium-Fat Meat, 2 Fat **Carbohydrate Choices:** 4

Bacon Pancakes with Maple–Peanut Butter Syrup

Prep Time: 35 Minutes • **Start to Finish:** 35 Minutes • **5 servings (3 pancakes)**

SYRUP

- 3 tablespoons peanut butter
- 1 tablespoon butter, softened
- ½ cup maple-flavored syrup

PANCAKES

- 2 cups Original Bisquick® mix
- ¾ cup milk
- ¼ cup maple-flavored syrup
- 2 eggs
- ½ cup real bacon pieces (from 3-oz package)

1 In small bowl, beat peanut butter and butter with electric mixer on low speed until smooth. Beat in ½ cup syrup until thoroughly mixed.

2 Heat nonstick griddle or 12-inch nonstick skillet over medium-low heat (350°F). Brush griddle with vegetable oil if necessary (or spray with cooking spray before heating).

3 In medium bowl, stir all pancake ingredients except bacon with whisk or fork until blended. Stir in bacon.

4 For each pancake, pour slightly less than ¼ cup batter onto hot griddle. Cook 2 to 3 minutes or until edges are dry. Turn; cook other side until golden brown. Serve pancakes with syrup.

1 Serving: Calories 510; Total Fat 19g (Saturated Fat 6g; Trans Fat 2g); Cholesterol 105mg; Sodium 900mg; Total Carbohydrate 71g (Dietary Fiber 2g); Protein 13g **Exchanges:** 2 Starch, 2½ Other Carbohydrate, 1 High-Fat Meat, 2 Fat **Carbohydrate Choices:** 5

Cheesecake Pancakes

Prep Time: 30 Minutes • **Start to Finish:** 8 Hours 30 Minutes • 5 servings (3 pancakes and 3 tablespoons syrup each)

PANCAKES

- 1 package (8 oz) cream cheese
- 2 cups Original Bisquick® mix
- ½ cup graham cracker crumbs
- ¼ cup sugar
- 1 cup milk
- 2 eggs

SYRUP

- 1 cup sliced fresh strawberries
- ½ cup strawberry syrup for pancakes

1 Slice cream cheese lengthwise into four pieces. Place on ungreased cookie sheet; cover. Freeze 8 hours or overnight.

2 Heat griddle or skillet over medium-high heat (375°F). Brush griddle with vegetable oil if necessary (or spray with cooking spray before heating).

3 Cut cream cheese into bite-size pieces; set aside. In large bowl, stir Bisquick mix, graham cracker crumbs, sugar, milk and eggs with whisk or fork until blended. Stir in cream cheese.

4 For each pancake, pour slightly less than ⅓ cup batter onto hot griddle. Cook until edges are dry. Turn; cook other side until golden brown.

5 In small bowl, mix strawberries and syrup; top pancakes with strawberry mixture.

1 Serving: Calories 580; Total Fat 26g (Saturated Fat 12g; Trans Fat 2.5g); Cholesterol 140mg; Sodium 830mg; Total Carbohydrate 75g (Dietary Fiber 2g); Protein 11g
Exchanges: 2½ Starch, 2½ Other Carbohydrate, ½ High-Fat Meat, 4 Fat **Carbohydrate Choices:** 5

> Use your favorite fruit, or offer a variety of fruits to top these pancakes.

Double Chocolate–Strawberry Pancakes

Prep Time: 40 Minutes • **Start to Finish:** 40 Minutes • 5 servings (3 pancakes each)

1½ cups Original Bisquick® mix

¼ cup unsweetened baking cocoa

1 container (8 oz) sour cream

½ cup milk

2 teaspoons strawberry extract or vanilla

2 eggs

1 cup semisweet chocolate chips (6 oz)

Whipped cream or frozen (thawed) whipped topping

2 cups sliced fresh strawberries

Strawberry syrup for pancakes

1 In large bowl, lightly stir Bisquick mix, cocoa, sour cream, milk, extract and eggs (do not overbeat; mixture should be lumpy). Fold in chocolate chips.

2 Heat griddle or 12-inch skillet over medium-high heat (375°F). Grease griddle with vegetable oil if necessary (or spray with cooking spray before heating).

3 For each pancake, pour slightly less than ¼ cup of batter onto hot griddle; spread batter with rubber spatula to 4 inches in diameter. Cook pancakes until bubbly on top, puffed and dry around edges, about 2 minutes. Turn; cook other sides until golden brown, about 1 to 2 minutes longer. Top with whipped cream, strawberries and syrup.

1 Serving: Calories 510; Total Fat 27g (Saturated Fat 14g, Trans Fat 1.5g); Cholesterol 110mg; Sodium 520mg; Total Carbohydrate 55g (Dietary Fiber 5g); Protein 9g **Exchanges:** 1 Starch, 1 Fruit, 1½ Other Carbohydrate, 1 High-Fat Meat, 4 Fat **Carbohydrate Choices:** 3½

These tasty pancakes are easy to make at the last minute. If you want to do a little prep ahead of time, cut up the strawberries the night before. The batter is somewhat thick; add more milk for thinner pancakes, if desired.

Christmas Tree Pancake Stacks

Prep Time: 10 Minutes • **Start to Finish:** 30 Minutes • 6 servings (1 pancake stack each)

PANCAKES

- 4 cups Original Bisquick® mix
- 2 cups milk
- 2 teaspoons green paste food color, if desired
- 4 eggs

GLAZE

- 2½ cups powdered sugar
- 3 tablespoons plus 2 teaspoons milk

GARNISHES, IF DESIRED

- Powdered sugar
- Candy sprinkles
- Small candies

1 In large bowl, stir all pancake ingredients until well blended.

2 Heat griddle or skillet over medium-high heat (375°F). Brush griddle with vegetable oil if necessary (or spray with cooking spray before heating).

3 Each pancake tree is a stack of 8 different-size pancakes. Make only one tree at a time. Pour ¼ cupful, 3 level measuring tablespoons, 2 level measuring tablespoons and 1 level measuring tablespoon batter onto hot griddle. Watching each pancake carefully, cook until bubbly on top and dry around edges (small pancakes will get done first). Turn; cook other side until light golden brown around edges. Keep warm. To make remaining 4 pancakes to form one tree, pour 2 level measuring teaspoons, 1 level measuring teaspoon, ½ level measuring teaspoon and ¼ level measuring teaspoon batter onto hot griddle. Watching each pancake carefully, cook until bubbly on top and dry around edges; pancakes will cook quickly. Turn; cook other side until light golden brown around edges (they will cook very quickly). Repeat with remaining batter to make 5 more trees.

4 To assemble trees, stack on serving plate starting with largest pancakes on bottom and stacking each smaller-size pancake on top. Drizzle with glaze or sprinkle with powdered sugar. Garnish with sprinkles and candies.

1 Serving: Calories 640; Total Fat 17g (Saturated Fat 5g; Trans Fat 2g); Cholesterol 130mg; Sodium 1070mg; Total Carbohydrate 107g (Dietary Fiber 2g); Protein 13g **Exchanges:** 2 Starch, 4½ Other Carbohydrate, ½ Low-Fat Milk, ½ Lean Meat, 2½ Fat **Carbohydrate Choices:** 7

Eggnog Pancakes with Maple-Butter-Rum Drizzle

Prep Time: 10 Minutes • **Start to Finish:** 20 Minutes • **14 servings**

DRIZZLE

¼ **cup butter**

½ **cup real maple syrup**

⅓ **cup whipping cream**

2 **tablespoons rum or
   ½ teaspoon rum extract**

PANCAKES

2 **cups Original
   Bisquick® mix**

2 **tablespoons sugar**

¼ **teaspoon ground nutmeg**

1 **cup eggnog**

2 **eggs**

TOPPINGS, IF DESIRED

**Sweetened
whipped cream**

Ground nutmeg

1 In 2-quart saucepan, melt butter over medium heat. Stir in remaining drizzle ingredients. Heat to boiling, stirring occasionally. Reduce heat; simmer 2 minutes, stirring frequently. Remove from heat. Cover; keep warm.

2 In large bowl, stir all pancake ingredients with whisk until well blended.

3 Heat griddle or skillet over medium-high heat (375°F). Brush griddle with vegetable oil if necessary (or spray with cooking spray before heating).

4 For each pancake, pour slightly less than ¼ cup batter onto hot griddle. Cook 2 to 3 minutes or until bubbles form on top and edges are dry. Turn; cook other side until light golden brown around edges. Serve pancakes with drizzle. Top with whipped cream; sprinkle with nutmeg.

1 Serving: Calories 200; Total Fat 10g (Saturated Fat 5g; Trans Fat 0.5g); Cholesterol 55mg; Sodium 280mg; Total Carbohydrate 24g (Dietary Fiber 0g); Protein 3g **Exchanges:** 1 Starch, ½ Other Carbohydrate, 2 Fat **Carbohydrate Choices:** 1½

Gingerbread Boy Pancakes

Prep Time: 20 Minutes • **Start to Finish:** 20 Minutes • 18 pancakes

PANCAKES

2½	cups Original Bisquick® mix
1	cup milk
¾	cup apple butter
2	tablespoons vegetable oil
¼	teaspoon ground cinnamon
¼	teaspoon ground ginger
¼	teaspoon ground nutmeg
2	eggs

TOPPINGS, IF DESIRED

1	can (6.4-oz) white decorating icing
	Small candies

1 In large bowl, stir all pancake ingredients with whisk until well blended.

2 Heat griddle or skillet over medium-high heat (375°F). Brush griddle with vegetable oil if necessary (or spray with cooking spray before heating).

3 For each pancake, pour ¼ cup batter onto hot griddle. Cook 2 to 3 minutes or until bubbles form on top and edges are dry. Turn; cook other side until golden brown.

4 Using 3½ to 4-inch gingerbread boy or girl cookie cutter, cut one shape from each warm pancake. Decorate as desired using icing and candies.

1 Pancake: Calories 120; Total Fat 5g (Saturated Fat 1g; Trans Fat 0g); Cholesterol 20mg; Sodium 220mg; Total Carbohydrate 17g (Dietary Fiber 0g); Protein 2g **Exchanges:** 1 Starch, 1 Fat **Carbohydrate Choices:** 1

Serving Ideas for Pancakes and Waffles

Bisquick pancakes are delicious just the way they are, drizzled with syrup. But sometimes that isn't enough to raise tired ones from their beds. If you want a fun and tasty way to wake up sleepyheads, try one of these topping variations or serving suggestions. Just a few ingredients can turn ho-hum into yum-yum!

Cinnamon Roll Topper—Heat ½ cup brown sugar, 2 tablespoons butter and ¼ teaspoon ground cinnamon until melted and smooth; drizzle about 2 tablespoons over each serving of pancakes or waffles. Then drizzle each serving with 2 to 3 tablespoons vanilla yogurt.

Strawberries 'n Cream Topper—Top waffles or pancakes with sliced fresh strawberries, 1 to 2 tablespoons strawberry pancake syrup and a spoonful of whipped cream.

Peanut Butter and Granola Topper—Top waffles or pancakes with 2 to 3 tablespoons peanut butter and 2 to 3 tablespoons granola.

Silver Dollar Stacks—Make mini-size pancakes or waffles using 1 to 2 tablespoons batter per pancake or waffle. Spread each of the pancakes or waffles with about 1 teaspoon each softened cream cheese and orange marmalade. Stack them up, 3 to 5 pancakes or waffles high; secure with a decorative toothpick. Top each stack with an orange slice.

Maple-Bacon Topper—Top pancakes or waffles with crumbled bacon and real maple syrup.

Banana-Walnut Topper—Layer sliced bananas, candied walnuts, and vanilla yogurt over pancakes or waffles.

Chorizo-Maple Pancakes—Top pancakes with cooked chorizo sausage and real maple syrup.

Egg-Topped Breakfast—Top each waffle with a fried egg and shredded Swiss cheese.

MAKE A PANCAKE OR WAFFLE BAR

Put out a top-your-own pancake or waffle bar the next time you entertain for breakfast or brunch, are in need of a creative birthday celebration or when hosting a team breakfast or sleepover. All you need are pancakes or waffles and a bunch of toppings and your favorite breakfast beverages. You can stop there or round out the meal with a breakfast egg bake such as Muffuletta Brunch Bake (page 188) or Overnight Chorizo and Egg Bake (page 193) and cooked bacon or sausage.

PANCAKE OR WAFFLE BAR TOPPINGS

Set up a delicious arrangement of any or all of these toppings for your guests to use to top their own waffles or pancakes:

- Fresh berries or bite-size pieces of fresh fruit
- Different flavors of pancake/waffle syrup
- Hot apple, cherry and blueberry pie fillings
- Hot fudge ice cream topping and chocolate and caramel sauces
- Peanut butter
- Fruit jams or preserves
- Softened plain or flavored cream cheese or cream-cheese frosting

- Chopped nuts
- Chocolate, peanut butter and butterscotch chips and toffee bits
- Crumbled, cooked bacon
- Assorted sprinkles
- Assorted small soft candies such as mini peanut butter cups and candy-coated chocolate candies
- Cinnamon-sugar
- Coconut
- Whipped cream
- Yogurt
- Granola cereal

Easy Berry Pancakes

Prep Time: 20 Minutes • **Start to Finish:** 20 Minutes • 9 pancakes

1¼ cups Original
     Bisquick® mix

  1 egg

⅔ cup milk

  2 tablespoons
     vegetable oil

  1 cup fresh blueberries

     Maple syrup or powdered
     sugar, if desired

     Sliced fresh strawberries,
     if desired

     Additional fresh
     blueberries, if desired

1 In medium bowl, stir Bisquick mix, egg, milk and oil with fork or whisk until blended. Gently stir in 1 cup blueberries.

2 Heat griddle or skillet over medium-high heat (375°F). Brush griddle with vegetable oil if necessary (or spray with cooking spray before heating).

3 For each pancake, pour about ¼ cup batter onto hot griddle. Cook until bubbles form on top and edges are dry. Turn; cook other side until golden brown.

4 Serve pancakes with syrup or powdered sugar. Top with strawberries and additional blueberries.

1 Pancake: Calories 120; Total Fat 6g (Saturated Fat 1g; Trans Fat 0g); Cholesterol 0mg; Sodium 223mg; Total Carbohydrate 14g (Dietary Fiber 1g); Protein 3g **Exchanges:** 1 Starch, 1 Fat **Carbohydrate Choices:** 1

Blackberry Yogurt Waffles

Prep Time: 25 Minutes • **Start to Finish:** 25 Minutes • 6 servings (1 waffle, 2 tablespoons yogurt and 2 tablespoons blackberries each)

WAFFLES

- 2 cups Original Bisquick® mix
- 1 cup fat-free (skim) milk
- 1 tablespoon vegetable oil
- 1 egg
- 1 container (6 oz) blackberry nonfat yogurt

TOPPING

- 1 container (6 oz) blackberry nonfat yogurt
- ¾ cup blackberries

1 Heat waffle maker. (Waffle makers without a nonstick coating may need to be brushed with vegetable oil or sprayed with cooking spray before batter for each waffle is added.)

2 In medium bowl, stir waffle ingredients until blended.

3 For each waffle, spread slightly less than ¾ cup batter onto center of hot waffle maker. (Waffle makers vary in size; check manufacturer's directions for recommended amount of batter.) Close lid of waffle maker.

4 Bake about 5 minutes or until steaming stops and waffle is golden brown. Carefully remove waffle. Repeat with remaining batter.

5 Top each waffle with about 2 tablespoons yogurt and 2 tablespoons blackberries.

1 Serving: Calories 250; Total Fat 8g (Saturated Fat 2g; Trans Fat 1.5g); Cholesterol 30mg; Sodium 540mg; Total Carbohydrate 36g (Dietary Fiber 2g); Protein 7g **Exchanges:** 1 Starch, 1 Other Carbohydrate, ½ Skim Milk, 1½ Fat **Carbohydrate Choices:** 2½

Gluten-Free Banana-Pecan Waffles

Prep Time: 35 Minutes • **Start to Finish:** 35 Minutes • 5 (6½-inch) waffles

WAFFLES

1⅓ cups Bisquick® Gluten Free mix

1¼ cups milk

3 tablespoons vegetable oil

1 egg

1 ripe medium banana, mashed

⅓ cup chopped pecans, toasted*

TOPPINGS, IF DESIRED

Real maple syrup

Sliced bananas

Additional chopped pecans, toasted*

1 In large bowl, stir Bisquick mix, milk, oil and egg with whisk or fork until blended. Gently stir in mashed banana and ⅓ cup pecans.

2 Heat waffle maker. (Waffle makers without a nonstick coating may need to be brushed with vegetable oil or sprayed with cooking spray before batter for each waffle is added.)

3 For each waffle, pour about ½ cup batter onto center of hot waffle maker. (Waffle makers vary in size; check manufacturer's directions for recommended amount of batter.) Close lid of waffle maker.

4 Bake about 5 minutes or until steaming stops and waffle is golden brown. Carefully remove waffle. Repeat with remaining batter. Serve with toppings.

*To toast pecans, cook in an ungreased skillet over medium heat 5 to 7 minutes, stirring frequently, until golden brown.

1 Waffle: Calories 310; Total Fat 16g (Saturated Fat 3g; Trans Fat 0g); Cholesterol 45mg; Sodium 400mg; Total Carbohydrate 37g (Dietary Fiber 2g); Protein 5g **Exchanges:** 1½ Starch, 1 Other Carbohydrate, 3 Fat **Carbohydrate Choices:** 2½

> If you are cooking gluten free, always read labels to make sure each recipe ingredient is gluten free. Products and ingredient sources can change.

Bacon, Cheddar and Basil Waffles with Tomato Jam

Prep Time: 40 Minutes • **Start to Finish:** 40 Minutes • **6 servings**

JAM

- 6 medium plum (Roma) tomatoes, seeded, chopped
- ¼ cup granulated sugar
- 2 tablespoons white wine vinegar
- 2 tablespoons butter
- 1 to 2 teaspoons hot pepper sauce
- ½ teaspoon salt

WAFFLES

- 2 cups Original Bisquick® mix
- 1⅓ cups milk
- 1 egg
- 2 tablespoons olive oil
- 4 slices bacon, crisply cooked, crumbled
- ½ cup shredded Cheddar cheese (2 oz)
- ⅓ cup chopped fresh basil leaves

1 In 12-inch skillet, heat jam ingredients to boiling over medium-high heat. Reduce heat. Simmer uncovered about 30 minutes, stirring occasionally, until thickened. Keep warm.

2 In large bowl, stir Bisquick mix, milk, egg and olive oil until well blended. Gently stir in bacon, cheese and basil.

3 Heat waffle maker. (Waffle makers without a nonstick coating may need to be brushed with vegetable oil or sprayed with cooking spray before batter for each waffle is added.)

4 For each waffle, pour ½ cup batter onto center of hot waffle maker. (Waffle makers vary in size; check manufacturer's directions for recommended amount of batter.) Close lid of waffle maker.

5 Bake 3 to 4 minutes or until steaming stops and waffle is golden brown. Carefully remove waffle. Serve immediately topped with tomato jam. Repeat with remaining batter.

1 Serving: Calories 400; Total Fat 21g (Saturated Fat 8g; Trans Fat 2g); Cholesterol 60mg; Sodium 960mg; Total Carbohydrate 41g (Dietary Fiber 2g); Protein 11g **Exchanges:** 2 Starch, 1 Other Carbohydrate, ½ High-Fat Meat, 3 Fat **Carbohydrate Choices:** 3

> Serve these waffles topped with a fried egg and sprinkled with chopped fresh basil.

Waffles Benedict

Prep Time: 40 Minutes • **Start to Finish:** 40 Minutes • **4 servings**

1 package (0.9 oz) hollandaise sauce mix

1 tablespoon lemon juice

¼ teaspoon dried tarragon leaves

2 cups Original Bisquick® mix

1⅓ cups buttermilk

½ cup shredded Parmesan cheese (2 oz)

2 tablespoons vegetable oil

5 eggs

½ teaspoon white vinegar

8 thin slices prosciutto (about 4 oz)

Chopped fresh chives, if desired

1 Make hollandaise sauce as directed on package, adding lemon juice and tarragon. Cover to keep warm. In medium bowl, stir Bisquick mix, buttermilk, cheese, oil and 1 of the eggs with fork or whisk until blended. Let stand 5 minutes.

2 Heat waffle maker. (Waffle makers without a nonstick coating may need to be brushed with vegetable oil or sprayed with cooking spray before batter for each waffle is added.)

3 For each waffle, pour batter onto center of hot waffle maker. (Waffle makers vary in size; check manufacturer's directions for recommended amount of batter.) Close lid of waffle maker.

4 Bake about 5 minutes or until steaming stops and waffle is golden brown. Carefully remove waffle.

5 Meanwhile, in 3-quart saucepan, heat 2 to 3 inches water to boiling. When the water comes to a rolling boil, reduce heat until water is just simmering (bubbles rise slowly and break just below the surface). Add vinegar.

6 Break remaining 4 eggs, one at a time, into custard cup. Holding cup close to the water's surface, carefully slip eggs into water. Cook 3 to 5 minutes or until whites and yolks are firm, not runny. Remove with slotted spoon.

7 To serve, stack 2 waffles; top with 2 slices prosciutto, 1 poached egg and desired amount of hollandaise sauce. Garnish with chives.

1 Serving: Calories 570; Total Fat 28g (Saturated Fat 9g; Trans Fat 0g); Cholesterol 0mg; Sodium 2184mg; Total Carbohydrate 51g (Dietary Fiber 2g); Protein 29g **Exchanges:** 2 Starch, 1½ Other Carbohydrate, 1 Medium-Fat Meat, 2 High-Fat Meat, ½ Fat **Carbohydrate Choices:** 3½

Ham 'n Cheese French Toast

Prep Time: 15 Minutes • **Start to Finish:** 15 Minutes • 6 servings (2 toast halves each)

1 cup milk

⅓ cup Original Bisquick® mix

2 teaspoons vanilla

4 eggs

6 slices (1 inch thick) day-old ciabatta or French bread

2 tablespoons Dijon mustard

6 oz thinly sliced cooked ham (from deli)

1½ cups shredded mild Cheddar cheese (6 oz)

2 tablespoons butter

Powdered sugar

1 In shallow dish, stir milk, Bisquick mix, vanilla and eggs with fork or whisk until blended. In each slice of bread, cut 3-inch pocket through top crust. Spread about 1 teaspoon mustard in each pocket. Place 1 oz ham and ¼ cup cheese in each pocket.

2 Heat griddle or skillet over medium heat (350°F). Melt butter on griddle. Dip bread into egg mixture, coating both sides. Place bread on hot griddle; cook about 5 minutes, turning once, until golden brown.

3 Cut French toast in half diagonally; sprinkle with powdered sugar.

1 Serving: Calories 390; Total Fat 21g (Saturated Fat 11g; Trans Fat 0.5g); Cholesterol 185mg; Sodium 980mg; Total Carbohydrate 26g (Dietary Fiber 1g); Protein 23g **Exchanges:** ½ Starch, 1 Other Carbohydrate, 1 Very Lean Meat, 1 Medium-Fat Meat, 1 High-Fat Meat, 1½ Fat **Carbohydrate Choices:** 2

For a sweet and savory taste, serve with your favorite jam or preserves.

Chocolate-Stuffed French Toast

Prep Time: 30 Minutes • **Start to Finish:** 30 Minutes • 6 servings (1 piece French toast and about 1 tablespoon orange butter each)

BUTTER

- ½ cup butter, softened
- 2 tablespoons powdered sugar
- 1 tablespoon grated orange peel

FRENCH TOAST

- 1 cup milk
- ⅓ cup Original Bisquick® mix
- 1 tablespoon vanilla
- 1 teaspoon grated orange peel
- 1 tablespoon fresh orange juice
- 4 eggs
- 6 slices (1 inch thick) day-old French bread
- 6 tablespoons hazelnut spread with cocoa
- 2 tablespoons butter

TOPPINGS, IF DESIRED

- Additional powdered sugar
- Additional hazelnut spread with cocoa

1 In small bowl, stir butter ingredients with wooden spoon until blended. Cover; refrigerate until serving time.

2 In shallow dish, stir milk, Bisquick mix, vanilla, 1 teaspoon orange peel, the orange juice and eggs with fork or whisk until blended. In each slice of bread, cut 3-inch pocket through top crust. Spread 1 tablespoon hazelnut spread in each pocket.

3 Heat griddle or skillet over medium heat (350°F). Melt 2 tablespoons butter on griddle. Dip bread in egg mixture, coating both sides. Place bread on hot griddle; cook about 4 minutes, turning once, until golden brown.

4 Sprinkle French toast with additional powdered sugar; top with additional hazelnut spread. Serve with orange butter.

1 Serving: Calories 477; Total Fat 30g (Saturated Fat 19g; Trans Fat 0g); Cholesterol 0mg; Sodium 490mg; Total Carbohydrate 40g (Dietary Fiber 2g); Protein 11g **Exchanges:** 1 Starch, 1½ Other Carbohydrate, 1 Medium-Fat Meat, 5 Fat **Carbohydrate Choices:** 3½

Cream Cheese–Filled Batter-Dipped French Toast

Prep Time: 35 Minutes • **Start to Finish:** 35 Minutes • 8 servings (1 sandwich each)

5 oz cream cheese, softened

¼ cup orange marmalade

16 diagonally cut slices (½ inch thick) French bread

1 cup Original Bisquick® mix

1 teaspoon ground cinnamon

½ teaspoon grated orange peel

⅔ cup milk

½ teaspoon vanilla

1 egg

1 tablespoon powdered sugar

Maple-flavored syrup, if desired

1 In small bowl, mix cream cheese and marmalade until blended. Spread 8 slices of the bread with cream cheese mixture. Top each with 1 of the remaining bread slices, making 8 sandwiches.

2 In shallow dish or pie pan, stir Bisquick mix, cinnamon, orange peel, milk, vanilla and egg with whisk or fork until blended.

3 Heat nonstick griddle or skillet over medium heat (350°F).

4 Dip each sandwich into batter, turning to coat both sides; drain excess batter into dish. Cook on hot griddle 1 to 2 minutes on each side or until golden brown. Sprinkle each sandwich with powdered sugar; serve with syrup.

1 Serving: Calories 550; Total Fat 11g (Saturated Fat 5g; Trans Fat 1g); Cholesterol 50mg; Sodium 1090mg; Total Carbohydrate 92g (Dietary Fiber 4g); Protein 18g **Exchanges:** 4 Starch, 1½ Other Carbohydrate, ½ Milk, 1 Fat **Carbohydrate Choices:** 6

Use English muffin bread or swirled cinnamon bread in place of the French bread.

Scrambled Egg Biscuit Cups

Prep Time: 30 Minutes • **Start to Finish:** 30 Minutes • **12 biscuit cups**

2 cups Original Bisquick® mix

⅓ cup shredded Cheddar cheese (1½ oz)

¾ cup milk

8 eggs

⅛ teaspoon pepper

1 tablespoon butter, softened

½ cup Parmesan and mozzarella cheese pasta sauce (from 1-lb jar)

3 tablespoons cooked real bacon bits or pieces (from 3-oz package)

1 tablespoon chopped fresh chives

Additional cooked real bacon bits or pieces

1 Heat oven to 425°F. Spray bottoms only of 12 regular-size muffin cups with cooking spray. In medium bowl, mix Bisquick mix, cheese and ½ cup of the milk until soft dough forms.

2 Place dough on surface sprinkled with Bisquick mix. Shape into a ball; knead 4 or 5 times. Shape into 10-inch-long roll. Cut roll into 12 pieces. Press each piece in bottom and up side of muffin cup, forming edge at rim.

3 Bake 8 to 10 minutes or until golden brown. Remove from oven. With back of spoon, press puffed crust in each cup to make indentation.

4 In large bowl, beat eggs, remaining ¼ cup milk and the pepper until well blended. In 10-inch nonstick skillet, melt butter over medium heat. Add egg mixture; cook 3 to 4 minutes, stirring occasionally, until firm but still moist. Fold in pasta sauce and bacon until blended.

5 To remove biscuit cups from pan, run knife around edge of cups. Spoon egg mixture into biscuit cups. Sprinkle chives and additional bacon bits over tops.

1 Biscuit Cup: Calories 180; Total Fat 9g (Saturated Fat 3.5g, Trans Fat 1g); Cholesterol 150mg; Sodium 420mg; Total Carbohydrate 15g (Dietary Fiber 0g); Protein 8g
Exchanges: 1 Starch, 1 Medium-Fat Meat, ½ Fat **Carbohydrate Choices:** 1

Biscuit cups can be baked the day before and stored in an airtight container at room temperature. Just fill with scrambled eggs and serve.

Mini Quiches

Prep Time: 35 Minutes • **Start to Finish:** 55 Minutes • 24 mini quiches

1¼ cups Original Bisquick® mix

¼ cup butter, softened

2 tablespoons boiling water

6 slices bacon, crisply cooked, crumbled

½ cup half-and-half

1 egg

2 tablespoons thinly sliced green onions (2 medium)

¼ teaspoon salt

¼ teaspoon ground red pepper (cayenne)

½ cup shredded Swiss cheese (2 oz)

1 Heat oven to 375°F. Spray 24 mini muffin cups with cooking spray.

2 In medium bowl, mix Bisquick mix and butter. Add boiling water; stir vigorously until soft dough forms. Press rounded teaspoonful dough on bottom and up side of each muffin cup. Divide bacon evenly among muffin cups.

3 In small bowl, beat half-and-half and egg until well blended. Beat in onions, salt and red pepper. Spoon 1½ teaspoons into each muffin cup; sprinkle with cheese.

4 Bake 18 to 20 minutes or until edges are golden brown and centers are set. Remove quiches from pan to cooling rack. Serve warm.

1 Mini Quiche: Calories 70; Total Fat 5g (Saturated Fat 2.5g; Trans Fat 0g); Cholesterol 20mg; Sodium 170mg; Total Carbohydrate 5g (Dietary Fiber 0g); Protein 2g **Exchanges:** ½ Other Carbohydrate, 1 Fat **Carbohydrate Choices:** ½

These bite-size quiches can be made one day ahead. Remove the baked quiches from the muffin pan and cool completely on a cooling rack. Cover tightly and store in the refrigerator. To serve, place on an ungreased cookie sheet and cover loosely with foil. Reheat in a 375°F oven about 10 minutes or until hot.

Breakfast Sausage Pies

Prep Time: 15 Minutes • **Start to Finish:** 1 Hour • **6 pies**

SAUSAGE MIXTURE

- ¾ lb bulk pork sausage
- 1 large onion, chopped (1 cup)
- 1 can (4 oz) mushroom pieces and stems, drained
- ½ teaspoon salt
- 3 tablespoons fresh sage, chopped
- 1 cup shredded Cheddar cheese (4 oz)

BAKING MIXTURE

- ¾ cup Original Bisquick® mix
- ¾ cup milk
- 3 eggs

1 Heat oven to 375°F. Spray 6 jumbo muffin cups with cooking spray.

2 In 10-inch skillet, cook sausage and onion over medium-high heat 5 to 7 minutes, stirring occasionally until sausage is no longer pink; drain. Let cool 5 minutes; stir in mushrooms, salt, sage and cheese.

3 In medium bowl, stir baking mixture ingredients with whisk or fork until blended. Spoon 3 tablespoons of baking mixture into each muffin cup. Top each with ½ cup sausage mixture and 2 tablespoons baking mixture.

4 Bake 27 to 30 minutes or until toothpick inserted in center comes out clean and tops of pies are golden brown. Cool 5 minutes. With thin knife, loosen sides of pies from pan. Remove pies from pan to cooling rack. Cool 10 minutes; serve warm.

1 Pie: Calories 300; Total Fat 19g (Saturated Fat 8g; Trans Fat 1g); Cholesterol 150mg; Sodium 820mg; Total Carbohydrate 15g (Dietary Fiber 1g); Protein 15g **Exchanges:** 1 Starch, 1½ Lean Meat, 3 Fat **Carbohydrate Choices:** 1

Tomato-Pesto Brunch Bake

Prep Time: 20 Minutes • **Start to Finish:** 1 Hour 5 Minutes • **12 servings**

2½ cups Original Bisquick® mix

½ cup grated Parmesan cheese

¾ cup milk

2 cups shredded mozzarella cheese (8 oz)

3 large tomatoes, cut into thin slices

½ cup refrigerated basil pesto

4 eggs

½ cup whipping cream

1 teaspoon salt

½ teaspoon white pepper

1 Heat oven to 350°F. In medium bowl, stir Bisquick mix, Parmesan cheese and milk until soft dough forms.

2 Using fingers coated in Bisquick mix, press dough in bottom and ½ inch up sides of ungreased 13x9-inch (3-quart) glass baking dish.

3 Sprinkle 1½ cups of the mozzarella cheese over crust. Layer tomatoes over cheese, overlapping if necessary. Spread pesto over tomatoes.

4 In medium bowl, beat eggs, whipping cream, salt and pepper with whisk or fork until blended. Gently pour mixture over tomatoes. Sprinkle with remaining ½ cup mozzarella cheese.

5 Bake 35 to 40 minutes or until top is golden brown. Let stand 5 minutes before serving. Cut into squares.

1 Serving: Calories 300; Total Fat 19g (Saturated Fat 8g; Trans Fat 1g); Cholesterol 100mg; Sodium 780mg; Total Carbohydrate 21g (Dietary Fiber 1g); Protein 12g **Exchanges:** 1 Starch, ½ Low-Fat Milk, ½ Vegetable, ½ Lean Meat, 3 Fat **Carbohydrate Choices:** 1½

Muffuletta Brunch Bake

Prep Time: 15 Minutes • **Start to Finish:** 1 Hour 15 Minutes • **12 servings**

BREAKFAST BAKE

- 8 oz thinly sliced Genoa salami
- 4 cups frozen shredded hash brown potatoes
- 1 jar (32 oz) giardiniera vegetable mix, drained, coarsely chopped
- ½ cup chopped pimiento-stuffed green olives
- 2½ cups shredded Colby–Monterey Jack cheese blend (10 oz)
- 2 cups milk
- 1 cup Original Bisquick® mix
- 1 teaspoon Italian seasoning
- 5 eggs

GARNISHES, IF DESIRED

Cornichons

Whole pimiento-stuffed (colossal queen) green olives

2 oz thinly sliced Genoa salami

1 Heat oven to 400°F. Grease 13x9-inch (3-quart) glass baking dish with shortening or cooking spray.

2 Arrange 8 oz salami, overlapping slightly, in bottom and halfway up sides of baking dish. Top with potatoes, vegetable mix, chopped olives and 1 cup of the cheese.

3 In medium bowl, stir milk, Bisquick mix, Italian seasoning and eggs with fork or whisk until blended. Pour over vegetable mixture.

4 Bake uncovered 40 to 45 minutes or until golden brown around edges and knife inserted in center comes out clean. Sprinkle with remaining 1½ cups cheese. Bake 5 minutes longer or until cheese is melted. Let stand 10 minutes before serving. Cut into squares. Serve whole olives, cornichons and 2 oz salami on frilled toothpicks as a garnish.

1 Serving: Calories 305; Total Fat 20g (Saturated Fat 9g; Trans Fat 0g); Cholesterol 0mg; Sodium 1392mg; Total Carbohydrate 17g (Dietary Fiber 1g); Protein 15g **Exchanges:** 1 Starch, 2 High-Fat Meat, 1 Fat **Carbohydrate Choices:** 1

Apple-Sausage-Cheddar Breakfast Bake

Prep Time: 25 Minutes • **Start to Finish:** 1 Hour 10 Minutes • 12 servings

2 packages (12 oz each) pork sausage links

1 can (21 oz) apple pie filling with more fruit

2 medium apples, peeled, chopped (about 2 cups)

2 cups shredded sharp Cheddar cheese (8 oz)

1½ cups Original Bisquick® mix

1½ cups milk

¼ teaspoon salt

⅛ teaspoon pepper

6 eggs

1 Heat oven to 375°F. Spray 13x9-inch (3-quart) glass baking dish with cooking spray.

2 In 12-inch skillet, cook sausage over medium-high heat 5 to 7 minutes, breaking up with spoon, until no longer pink; drain. Stir in pie filling and apples. Spread mixture evenly in baking dish. Top with 1 cup of the cheese.

3 In large bowl, stir Bisquick mix, milk, salt, pepper and eggs with whisk or fork until blended. Pour evenly over cheese.

4 Bake 30 to 37 minutes or until knife inserted in center comes out clean. Top with remaining 1 cup cheese. Bake 3 to 5 minutes longer or until cheese is melted. Let stand 5 minutes before serving. Cut into squares.

1 Serving: Calories 340; Total Fat 19g (Saturated Fat 8g; Trans Fat 1g); Cholesterol 150mg; Sodium 590mg; Total Carbohydrate 28g (Dietary Fiber 1g); Protein 15g **Exchanges:** 1 Starch, 1 Other Carbohydrate, 1½ High-Fat Meat, 1 Fat **Carbohydrate Choices:** 2

> **This bake can be made 8 to 12 hours ahead. Make as directed through step 3; cover and refrigerate. When ready to bake continue as directed in step 4 (bake time may be longer).**

Cheddar and Potatoes Breakfast Bake

Prep Time: 10 Minutes • **Start to Finish:** 55 Minutes • 12 servings

4 cups frozen potatoes O'Brien with onions and peppers (from 28-oz bag), thawed

1½ cups shredded reduced-fat Cheddar cheese (6 oz)

5 slices fully cooked turkey bacon, chopped

1 cup Bisquick Heart Smart® mix

3 cups fat-free (skim) milk

1 cup fat-free egg product

½ teaspoon pepper

1 Heat oven to 375°F. Spray 13x9-inch (3-quart) glass baking dish with cooking spray.

2 In medium bowl, mix uncooked potatoes, 1 cup of the cheese and the bacon. Spread in baking dish.

3 In same bowl, stir Bisquick mix, milk, egg product and pepper until blended. Pour over potato mixture. Sprinkle with remaining ½ cup cheese.

4 Bake 30 to 35 minutes or until light golden brown around edges and cheese is melted. Let stand 10 minutes before serving. Cut into squares.

1 Serving: Calories 140; Total Fat 3.5g (Saturated Fat 1g; Trans Fat 0g); Cholesterol 10mg; Sodium 430mg; Total Carbohydrate 17g (Dietary Fiber 0g); Protein 10g **Exchanges:** 1 Starch, 1 Lean Meat **Carbohydrate Choices:** 1

This recipe can be made 8 to 12 hours ahead. Make as directed through step 2, except do not sprinkle with the ½ cup of remaining cheese; cover and refrigerate. When ready to bake, continue as directed in step 3, sprinkling with remaining ½ cup cheese (bake time may be longer).

Overnight Chorizo and Egg Bake

Prep Time: 20 Minutes • **Start to Finish:** 9 Hours 25 Minutes • 6 servings

1 lb bulk chorizo sausage
   or pork sausage

1 cup Original
   Bisquick® mix

1 cup shredded pepper
   Jack cheese (4 oz)

2 cups milk

2 teaspoons chopped
   fresh cilantro

1 teaspoon
   ground mustard

6 eggs, slightly beaten

   Chunky-style salsa, if
   desired

1 Spray 8-inch square (2-quart) glass baking dish with cooking spray.

2 In 10-inch skillet, cook sausage over medium-high heat 5 to 7 minutes, stirring occasionally, until no longer pink; drain.

3 In large bowl, mix sausage and remaining ingredients except salsa. Pour into baking dish. Cover; refrigerate at least 8 hours but no longer than 24 hours.

4 Heat oven to 350°F. Bake uncovered 50 to 60 minutes or until knife inserted in center comes out clean. Let stand 5 minutes before serving. Cut into squares. Serve with salsa.

1 Serving: Calories 510; Total Fat 36g (Saturated Fat 13g; Trans Fat 0.5g); Cholesterol 300mg; Sodium 1080mg; Total Carbohydrate 17g (Dietary Fiber 0g); Protein 29g **Exchanges:** ½ Starch, ½ Other Carbohydrate, 4 Medium-Fat Meat, 3 Fat **Carbohydrate Choices:** 1

> Serve with raspberry muffins and fresh orange juice.
>
> Try substituting 1 cup shredded Mexican-style taco-flavored cheese for the pepper Jack cheese.

Impossibly Easy Chorizo Breakfast Bake

Prep Time: 25 Minutes • **Start to Finish:** 55 Minutes • **6 servings**

BREAKFAST BAKE

- 1 lb bulk chorizo sausage
- 1 small yellow onion, diced
- 2 cloves garlic, finely chopped
- 1 can (15 oz) black beans, drained, rinsed
- 2 cups shredded Monterey Jack cheese (8 oz)
- ¾ cup Original Bisquick® mix
- 1½ cups milk
- 3 eggs
- 1 tablespoon chopped fresh cilantro

GARNISHES, IF DESIRED

- Sliced fresh avocado
- Chopped fresh tomato
- Salsa
- Hot sauce
- Lime wedges

1 Heat oven to 400°F. In 10-inch cast-iron or other ovenproof skillet, cook sausage, onion and garlic 5 to 7 minutes over medium-high heat, stirring occasionally, until sausage is no longer pink and onion is tender; drain.

2 Reserve ¾ cup of the black beans; stir remaining black beans into sausage mixture in skillet. Stir in 1 cup of the cheese.

3 In medium bowl, stir Bisquick mix, milk and eggs until blended. Pour over sausage mixture in skillet. Top with reserved black beans and remaining 1 cup cheese.

4 Bake 25 to 30 minutes or until knife inserted in center comes out clean. Cool 5 minutes. Top with chopped cilantro. Cut into wedges. Serve with garnishes.

1 Serving: Calories 690; Total Fat 47g (Saturated Fat 20g; Trans Fat 1g); Cholesterol 200mg; Sodium 1590mg; Total Carbohydrate 30g (Dietary Fiber 6g); Protein 38g **Exchanges:** 1½ Starch, 1 Vegetable, 1 Very Lean Meat, 1½ Medium-Fat Meat, 2 High-Fat Meat, 4½ Fat **Carbohydrate Choices:** 2

> For extra spice, add a seeded chopped jalapeño chile when cooking the onion and chorizo.
>
> To make this recipe ahead, prepare as directed through step 3. Cover and refrigerate up to 12 hours. Uncover, and bake as directed in step 4. (Bake time may be a bit longer.)

Pepperoni Breakfast Pizza

Prep Time: 20 Minutes • **Start to Finish:** 25 Minutes • 8 servings

1½ cups Original Bisquick® mix

⅓ cup hot water

8 eggs

¼ cup milk

⅛ teaspoon pepper

1 cup diced pepperoni (from 6-oz package)

2 medium green onions, sliced (2 tablespoons)

1 tablespoon butter

½ cup pizza sauce (from 8-oz can)

1½ cups finely shredded Italian cheese blend (6 oz)

1 tablespoon sliced fresh basil leaves, if desired

1 Heat oven to 425°F. Spray 12-inch pizza pan with cooking spray.

2 In medium bowl, stir Bisquick mix and hot water until soft dough forms. With fingers dipped in Bisquick mix, press dough in bottom and up side of pan forming rim at edge.

3 Bake 10 to 15 minutes or until golden brown.

4 Meanwhile, in large bowl, beat eggs, milk and pepper with whisk or fork until blended. Stir in pepperoni and onions. In 12-inch nonstick skillet, melt butter over medium heat. Add egg mixture; cook 3 to 5 minutes, stirring occasionally, until firm but still moist.

5 Spread pizza sauce over partially baked crust. Top evenly with egg mixture. Sprinkle with cheese. Bake 3 to 5 minutes longer or until cheese is melted and pizza is hot. Sprinkle with basil.

1 Serving: Calories 320; Total Fat 21g (Saturated Fat 9g, Trans Fat 1g); Cholesterol 245mg; Sodium 790mg; Total Carbohydrate 18g (Dietary Fiber 1g); Protein 16g **Exchanges:** 1 Starch, 2 Medium-Fat Meat, 2 Fat **Carbohydrate Choices:** 1

As with any pizza, it's easy to swap the toppings for your family's favorite. Cooked sausage, olives or your favorite cheese are just a few options you may want to try.

Basil leaves that are cut into thin strips are called "chiffonade." To cut, stack the leaves on top of each other, then roll them up like a cigar. Slice across the roll to form long shreds.

CHAPTER 4

Time for Dinner

Caprese Pizza with Crispy Pancetta

Prep Time: 30 Minutes • **Start to Finish:** 1 Hour • 8 servings

1 tablespoon yellow cornmeal

1½ cups Original Bisquick® mix

1½ teaspoons Italian seasoning

⅓ cup hot water

1 tablespoon olive oil

⅓ cup refrigerated basil pesto

3 medium tomatoes, cut into ¼-inch slices

8 oz fresh mozzarella cheese, cut into ¼-inch slices, or 1½ cups shredded mozzarella cheese (6 oz)

2 oz sliced pancetta or bacon, crisply cooked, crumbled

¼ cup fresh basil leaves, torn

3 tablespoons balsamic vinegar

1 Heat oven to 350°F. Spray 12-inch pizza pan with cooking spray; sprinkle with cornmeal.

2 In medium bowl, stir Bisquick mix, Italian seasoning, hot water and oil until soft dough forms. Place on surface lightly sprinkled with additional Bisquick mix; knead until smooth. Press dough in pizza pan. Bake 10 minutes.

3 Spread pesto over warm crust. Arrange tomatoes and mozzarella in circles on top of pesto, overlapping tomato and cheese slices. Bake 15 to 20 minutes longer or until crust is golden brown and cheese is melted. Sprinkle with pancetta and basil. Drizzle with balsamic vinegar. Cut into wedges.

1 Serving: Calories 300; Total Fat 19g (Saturated Fat 7g, Trans Fat 0g); Cholesterol 0mg; Sodium 700mg; Total Carbohydrate 20g (Dietary Fiber 1g); Protein 13g **Exchanges:** 1 Starch, ½ Low-Fat Milk, ½ Lean Meat, 2½ Fat **Carbohydrate Choices:** 1

> Sprinkling the pizza pan with cornmeal after spraying adds to the crispness of the crust.

Mediterranean Pizza

Prep Time: 25 Minutes • **Start to Finish:** 30 Minutes • 12 servings

CRUST

- 1½ cups Original Bisquick® mix
- ⅓ cup very hot water
- 1 tablespoon olive oil

DRESSING

- ½ cup red wine vinegar
- 3 cloves garlic, finely chopped
- 1 tablespoon dried basil leaves
- 1 teaspoon dried oregano leaves
- 3 tablespoons fresh lemon juice
- ¾ cup olive oil

TOPPINGS

- 2 packages (8 oz each) cream cheese, softened
- ½ cup diced sun-dried tomatoes in oil (from 8-oz jar)
- 1 cup chopped tomato
- 1 cup chopped cucumber
- ¼ cup chopped red onion
- ¼ cup sliced pitted kalamata olives
- 1 cup chopped fresh spinach
- ½ cup crumbled feta cheese (2 oz)

1 Heat oven to 400°F. Spray 12-inch pizza pan with cooking spray.

2 In medium bowl, stir crust ingredients until soft dough forms. With fingers dipped in Bisquick mix, press dough in bottom and up side of pan, forming rim at edge. Prick bottom with fork.

3 Bake 12 to 16 minutes or until crust is golden brown. Cool 10 minutes.

4 Meanwhile, in medium bowl, beat dressing ingredients with whisk until well blended. Set aside.

5 In medium bowl, mix cream cheese and sun-dried tomatoes. Spread mixture on warm crust. Top with tomato, cucumber, onion, olives and spinach. In small bowl, mix ¼ cup of the dressing and the feta cheese; spoon over pizza. Cut into wedges. (Cover and refrigerate remaining dressing for another use.)

1 Serving: Calories 380; Total Fat 32g (Saturated Fat 10g; Trans Fat 1g); Cholesterol 40mg; Sodium 540mg; Total Carbohydrate 17g (Dietary Fiber 1g); Protein 5g **Exchanges:** ½ Other Carbohydrate, 1 Low-Fat Milk, 5 Fat **Carbohydrate Choices:** 1

Mediterranean Pizza is a 2013 Bisquick Family Favorites Recipe Contest award-winning recipe developed by Elaine Mason of Oconomowoc, 2nd Place, Wisconsin State Fair (Milwaukee, WI).

Deep Dish Pizza Pie

Prep Time: 20 Minutes • **Start to Finish:** 1 Hour • 8 servings

1 lb bulk reduced-fat Italian pork sausage

1 large onion, chopped (1 cup)

1 small green bell pepper, chopped

2 cups Original Bisquick® mix

½ cup stone-ground yellow cornmeal

½ cup shredded Parmesan cheese (2 oz)

6 tablespoons cold butter

¼ cup boiling water

6 slices (¾ oz each) mozzarella cheese

⅔ cup pizza sauce

3 oz sliced pepperoni

2 cups shredded mozzarella cheese (8 oz)

Small fresh basil leaves, if desired

Additional pizza sauce, heated, if desired

1 Heat oven to 350°F. Spray 10-inch ovenproof skillet with cooking spray.

2 In 12-inch ovenproof skillet, cook sausage over medium heat, stirring frequently, until no longer pink. Remove sausage to paper towels; reserve drippings in skillet. Cook onion and bell pepper in drippings over medium heat, stirring frequently, until crisp-tender.

3 In medium bowl, mix Bisquick mix, cornmeal and Parmesan cheese. Cut in butter, using pastry blender or fork, until mixture looks like coarse crumbs. Add boiling water; stir vigorously until dough forms. Press dough in bottom and up side of skillet. Arrange mozzarella cheese slices over dough; spread with ⅓ cup of the pizza sauce. Top with sausage and onion mixture. Arrange two-thirds of the pepperoni over onion mixture. Spread remaining ⅓ cup pizza sauce over pepperoni; top with shredded mozzarella cheese and remaining pepperoni.

4 Bake 30 to 35 minutes or until crust is golden brown. Let stand 5 minutes before serving. Garnish with basil. Cut into wedges. Serve with pizza sauce.

1 Serving: Calories 585; Total Fat 39g (Saturated Fat 19g; Trans Fat 0g); Cholesterol 0mg; Sodium 506mg; Total Carbohydrate 34g (Dietary Fiber 2g); Protein 30g **Exchanges:** 1½ Starch, ½ Vegetable, 2 Medium-Fat Meat, 2 Fat **Carbohydrate Choices:** 1½

Stuffed-Crust Pizza

Prep Time: 20 Minutes • **Start to Finish:** 35 Minutes • 8 servings

3 cups Original Bisquick® mix

⅔ cup very hot water

2 tablespoons olive or vegetable oil

2 sticks part-skim mozzarella or Colby–Monterey Jack cheese (from 10-oz package), cut lengthwise in half

1 can (8 oz) pizza sauce

¾ cup shredded part-skim mozzarella cheese (3 oz)

2 cups sliced fresh mushrooms (6 oz)

1 cup chopped green bell pepper

1 can (2.25 oz) sliced ripe black olives, drained

1 Move oven rack to lowest position. Heat oven to 450°F. Spray 12-inch pizza pan with cooking spray.

2 In large bowl, stir Bisquick mix, hot water and oil with fork until soft dough forms; beat vigorously 20 strokes. If dough is dry, stir in additional 1 tablespoon water. Cover; let stand 8 minutes.

3 Press dough in bottom and 1 inch over side of pizza pan. Place sticks of cheese around edge of dough, overlapping if necessary. Fold 1-inch edge of dough over and around cheese; press to seal.

4 Bake 7 minutes or until very light golden brown. Remove from oven. Spread pizza sauce over partially baked crust. Sprinkle with ½ cup of the shredded cheese, the mushrooms, bell pepper and olives. Sprinkle with remaining ¼ cup shredded cheese.

5 Bake 9 to 12 minutes longer or until crust is golden brown and cheese is melted. Cut into wedges.

1 Serving: Calories 300; Total Fat 14g (Saturated Fat 4.5g; Trans Fat 2g); Cholesterol 10mg; Sodium 740mg; Total Carbohydrate 35g (Dietary Fiber 2g); Protein 9g **Exchanges:** 2 Starch, 1 Vegetable, ½ Lean Meat, 2 Fat **Carbohydrate Choices:** 2

Mini Monte Cristo Sandwiches

Prep Time: 15 Minutes • **Start to Finish:** 50 Minutes • **12 mini sandwiches**

SANDWICHES

- 2 cups Bisquick Heart Smart® mix
- ¾ cup fat-free (skim) milk
- 1 egg
- 6 oz thinly sliced reduced-fat Swiss cheese
- 6 oz thinly sliced cooked ham (from deli)
- 6 oz thinly sliced lean turkey (from deli)
- ¼ cup seedless raspberry jam

DIP

- 2 tablespoons seedless raspberry jam
- 1 container (6 oz) red raspberry nonfat yogurt

1 Heat oven to 400°F. Lightly spray 8-inch square (2-quart) glass baking dish with cooking spray.

2 In medium bowl, stir Bisquick mix, milk and egg until soft dough forms. Spread half of the dough in bottom of baking dish. Top with half each of the cheese, ham and turkey. Spread ¼ cup raspberry jam to within ½ inch of edges. Top with remaining cheese, ham and turkey. Spread remaining dough over turkey to sides of dish.

3 Bake 25 to 30 minutes or until golden brown. Let stand 5 minutes. For mini sandwiches, cut into 4 rows by 3 rows.

4 Meanwhile, in small bowl, stir dip ingredients until blended. Serve sandwiches with dip.

1 Mini Sandwich: Calories 160; Total Fat 3.5g (Saturated Fat 1g; Trans Fat 0g); Cholesterol 35mg; Sodium 560mg; Total Carbohydrate 20g (Dietary Fiber 0g); Protein 12g
Exchanges: 1½ Starch, 1 Lean Meat **Carbohydrate Choices:** 1

Monte Cristo sandwiches are traditionally dipped in batter and sautéed in butter—ours are much easier but just as tasty. The sandwiches are small, so for hungry appetites, serve two each!

BBQ Beef and Biscuit Sandwiches

Prep Time: 25 Minutes • **Start to Finish:** 8 Hours 40 Minutes • 16 sandwiches

BEEF

- 1 boneless beef rump roast (4 lb)
- 2 cups barbecue sauce
- 1 bottle (12 oz) dark beer

COLESLAW

- 1 container (6 oz) Greek fat-free plain yogurt
- ¼ cup mayonnaise
- 1 tablespoon sugar
- 3 tablespoons apple cider vinegar
- ¼ teaspoon salt
- 4 cups thinly sliced cabbage
- 2 tablespoons chopped green onions (2 medium)

BISCUITS

- 2 pouches (7.75 oz each) Bisquick® Complete cheese-garlic biscuits mix

1 Spray 4- to 5-quart slow cooker with cooking spray. Place beef in slow cooker. In small bowl, mix barbecue sauce and beer; pour over beef. Cover; cook on Low heat setting 8 to 10 hours or until beef is tender.

2 Meanwhile, in large bowl, mix yogurt, mayonnaise, sugar, vinegar and salt until smooth. Stir in cabbage and green onions. Cover; refrigerate until ready to serve.

3 About 30 minutes before serving, remove beef from slow cooker; place on cutting board. Shred beef with 2 forks; return to slow cooker to keep warm.

4 Heat oven to 450°F. Make and bake biscuits as directed on pouches, making 8 biscuits per package.

5 To serve, split biscuits in half. For each sandwich, spoon about ½ cup beef mixture onto bottom half of biscuit. Top beef with about 3 tablespoons coleslaw and top half of biscuit. Serve immediately.

1 Sandwich: Calories 340; Total Fat 11g (Saturated Fat 3.5g; Trans Fat 2g); Cholesterol 65mg; Sodium 690mg; Total Carbohydrate 32g (Dietary Fiber 0g); Protein 27g **Exchanges:** 1½ Starch, ½ Other Carbohydrate, ½ Vegetable, 2 Lean Meat, 1 Medium-Fat Meat **Carbohydrate Choices:** 2

Ham and String Cheese Roll-Ups

Prep Time: 15 Minutes • **Start to Finish:** 45 Minutes • 4 roll-ups

2 cups Original Bisquick® mix

¼ cup water

1 egg

2 teaspoons honey mustard

4 sticks (1 oz each) string cheese

8 slices (about 1 oz each) thinly sliced cooked ham (from deli)

1 tablespoon milk

1 Heat oven to 375°F. In medium bowl, stir Bisquick mix, water and egg until dough forms. Place dough on surface sprinkled with Bisquick mix; gently roll in Bisquick mix to coat. Knead 10 times. Divide dough into quarters.

2 For each roll-up, place one piece of dough on surface sprinkled with Bisquick mix; roll in Bisquick mix to coat. Pat or roll into 6½x4½-inch rectangle, ¼ inch thick.

3 Spread each dough rectangle with ½ teaspoon mustard. Wrap each cheese stick with 2 slices ham. Place ham and cheese bundle in center of dough. Bring dough up over bundle; pinch to seal. Pinch ends and tuck under. On ungreased cookie sheet, place roll-ups seam side down. Brush with milk.

4 Bake 18 to 23 minutes or until crust is golden brown. Let stand 5 minutes before serving.

1 Roll-Up: Calories 320; Total Fat 10g (Saturated Fat 3g; Trans Fat 0g); Cholesterol 75mg; Sodium 1080mg; Total Carbohydrate 42g (Dietary Fiber 0g); Protein 16g **Exchanges:** 2 Starch, 1 Other Carbohydrate, 1½ Medium-Fat Meat **Carbohydrate Choices:** 3

Hot Dog Rolls

Prep Time: 15 Minutes • **Start to Finish:** 30 Minutes • 8 servings

1¾ cups Original
    Bisquick® mix

⅓ cup milk

1 tablespoon
    yellow mustard

3 tablespoons pickle relish,
    drained

2 slices American cheese,
    each cut into 4 strips

8 hot dogs

Additional pickle relish, if
    desired

1 Heat oven to 425°F. Grease cookie sheet with shortening.

2 In medium bowl, stir Bisquick mix, milk and mustard until soft dough forms; beat 30 seconds. Place dough on surface sprinkled with Bisquick mix; gently roll in Bisquick mix to coat. Knead 10 times.

3 Roll or pat dough into 13-inch round; cut into 8 wedges. Place about 1 teaspoon pickle relish and 1 cheese strip along shortest side of each wedge about 1 inch from edge. Top with hot dog. Roll up, starting at shortest side of each wedge and rolling to opposite point; place point side down on cookie sheet.

4 Bake 10 to 12 minutes or until golden brown. Serve with additional pickle relish.

1 Serving: Calories 290; Total Fat 19g (Saturated Fat 7g; Trans Fat 1g); Cholesterol 30mg; Sodium 1010mg; Total Carbohydrate 22g (Dietary Fiber 0g); Protein 8g **Exchanges:** ½ Starch, 1 Other Carbohydrate, 1 High-Fat Meat, 2 Fat **Carbohydrate Choices:** 1½

> To grease the cookie sheet, use a pastry brush or paper towel to spread the shortening.

Beef and Spicy Sausage Foldovers

Prep Time: 25 Minutes • **Start to Finish:** 50 Minutes • 6 foldovers

½ lb lean (at least 80%) ground beef

½ lb bulk spicy Italian pork sausage

1 package (1 oz) taco seasoning mix

1 can (14.5 oz) diced tomatoes with green chiles, undrained

4½ cups Original Bisquick® mix

1 cup boiling water

1 cup shredded Mexican cheese blend (4 oz)

¾ cup sour cream

¾ cup chunky-style salsa

Fresh cilantro sprigs, if desired

1 Heat oven to 400°F. Grease large cookie sheet with shortening or cooking spray.

2 In 10-inch skillet, cook beef and sausage over medium-high heat 5 to 7 minutes, stirring occasionally, until thoroughly cooked; drain. Stir in taco seasoning mix and tomatoes. Reduce heat to medium; cook 5 minutes, stirring occasionally.

3 Meanwhile, in large bowl, stir Bisquick mix and boiling water with fork until dough forms. Place dough on surface sprinkled with Bisquick mix; gently roll dough in Bisquick mix to coat. Knead 20 times. Divide dough into 6 balls, about ½ cup each. Roll or pat each ball into 7-inch round.

4 Stir cheese into beef mixture. Spoon about ½ cup beef mixture onto half of each round to within ½ inch of edge. Moisten edge of each round with water. Fold each round in half, covering beef mixture. Press edges with tines of fork to seal. Cut 3 small slits in top of each foldover to allow steam to escape. With spatula, carefully place foldovers on cookie sheet.

5 Bake 20 to 22 minutes or until light golden brown. Serve each foldover with 2 tablespoons each sour cream and salsa. Garnish with cilantro.

1 Foldover: Calories 650; Total Fat 33g (Saturated Fat 13g; Trans Fat 2.5g); Cholesterol 75mg; Sodium 2550mg; Total Carbohydrate 66g (Dietary Fiber 2g); Protein 22g **Exchanges:** 2½ Starch, 2 Other Carbohydrate, 2 High-Fat Meat, 3 Fat **Carbohydrate Choices:** 4½

> **Make an extra batch of foldovers and freeze it. They are great to reheat for grab-and-go lunch or dinner.**

Impossibly Easy Mini Crab Cake Pies

Prep Time: 15 Minutes • **Start to Finish:** 1 Hour 5 Minutes • 6 servings (2 mini pies and 2 rounded tablespoons aioli each)

CRAB MIXTURE

- 2 cans (6 oz) crabmeat, drained, flaked
- ½ teaspoon seafood seasoning
- 1 tablespoon vegetable oil
- 1 medium onion, chopped (½ cup)
- ½ cup chopped red bell pepper
- ½ cup chopped green bell pepper
- 1 cup shredded mozzarella cheese (4 oz)

BAKING MIXTURE

- ½ cup Original Bisquick® mix
- ½ cup milk
- 2 eggs

AIOLI

- ½ cup mayonnaise
- ½ teaspoon seafood seasoning
- 1 tablespoon fresh lemon juice

1 Heat oven to 375°F. Spray 12 regular-size muffin cups with cooking spray. In small bowl, mix crabmeat and ½ teaspoon seafood seasoning; set aside.

2 In 10-inch skillet, heat oil over medium-high heat. Add onion and bell peppers; cook 4 minutes, stirring frequently. Add crabmeat mixture; cook and stir until thoroughly heated. Cool 5 minutes; stir in cheese.

3 In medium bowl, stir baking mixture ingredients with whisk or fork until blended. Spoon scant 1 tablespoon baking mixture into each muffin cup. Top each with about ¼ cup crab mixture and 1 tablespoon baking mixture.

4 Bake 30 to 35 minutes or until toothpick inserted in center comes out clean and tops are golden brown. Cool 5 minutes. With thin knife, loosen sides of pies from pan; remove to cooling rack. Cool 10 minutes.

5 Meanwhile, in small bowl, mix aioli ingredients. Serve each mini pie topped with a rounded tablespoonful of aioli.

1 Serving: Calories 340; Total Fat 24g (Saturated Fat 6g; Trans Fat 0.5g); Cholesterol 120mg; Sodium 660mg; Total Carbohydrate 12g (Dietary Fiber 1g); Protein 16g **Exchanges:** ½ Starch, ½ Other Carbohydrate, 1½ Very Lean Meat, ½ Medium-Fat Meat, 4 Fat **Carbohydrate Choices:** 1

Impossibly Easy Mexican Mini Veggie Pies

Prep Time: 20 Minutes • **Start to Finish:** 1 Hour 15 Minutes • 6 servings (2 mini pies each)

VEGGIE MIXTURE

- 1 tablespoon vegetable oil
- 1 large onion, chopped (1 cup)
- 1 to 2 chipotle chiles in adobo sauce (from 7-oz can), chopped
- ½ cup frozen corn, thawed
- 2 cloves garlic, finely chopped
- ¼ teaspoon dried oregano leaves
- ½ teaspoon salt
- 1 tablespoon fresh lime juice
- 1 cup canned black beans, drained, rinsed
- ¼ cup fresh cilantro, chopped
- 1 cup shredded Cheddar cheese (4 oz)

BAKING MIXTURE

- ½ cup Original Bisquick® mix
- ½ cup milk
- 2 eggs

GARNISHES, IF DESIRED

- 1 pint cherry or grape tomatoes, cut in half
- 1 avocado, pitted, peeled and chopped

1 Heat oven to 375°F. Spray 12 regular-size muffin cups with cooking spray.

2 In 10-inch skillet, heat oil over medium-high heat. Add onion, chiles, corn and garlic; cook 5 minutes, stirring occasionally. Add oregano, salt, lime juice, beans and cilantro; stir until combined. Remove from heat. Cool 5 minutes; stir in cheese.

3 In medium bowl, stir baking mixture ingredients with whisk or fork until blended. Spoon scant 1 tablespoon baking mixture into each muffin cup. Top each with about ¼ cup veggie mixture and 1 tablespoon baking mixture.

4 Bake 30 to 35 minutes or until toothpick inserted in center comes out clean and tops are golden brown. Cool 5 minutes. With thin knife, loosen sides of pies from pan; remove from pan to cooling rack. Cool 10 minutes. Serve with garnishes.

1 Serving: Calories 350; Total Fat 22g (Saturated Fat 9g; Trans Fat 0.5g); Cholesterol 100mg; Sodium 650mg; Total Carbohydrate 27g (Dietary Fiber 6g); Protein 13g **Exchanges:** 1 Starch, ½ Other Carbohydrate, 1 Vegetable, ½ Very Lean Meat, ½ High-Fat Meat, 3½ Fat **Carbohydrate Choices:** 2

For a little less spiciness, substitute 1 teaspoon ground cumin for the chipotle chiles.

To quickly thaw frozen corn, place in a colander or strainer; rinse with warm water until thawed. Drain well.

Impossibly Easy Macaroni and Cheese Pie

Prep Time: 15 Minutes • **Start to Finish:** 1 Hour 10 Minutes • **6 servings**

3 cups shredded Cheddar cheese (12 oz)

1 cup cubed cooked ham

1 cup uncooked elbow macaroni (3½ oz)

2¼ cups milk

2 eggs

½ cup Original Bisquick® mix

¼ teaspoon salt

Chopped fresh parsley, if desired

1 Heat oven to 400°F. Spray 10 or 9½-inch glass deep-dish pie plate with cooking spray.

2 In large bowl, mix 2 cups of the cheese, the ham and macaroni. Spread in pie plate.

3 In blender, place milk and eggs. Cover; blend on medium speed until smooth. Add Bisquick mix and salt. Cover; blend until smooth. Pour over mixture in pie plate.

4 Bake 35 to 40 minutes or until knife inserted in center comes out clean. Sprinkle with remaining 1 cup cheese. Bake 1 to 2 minutes longer or until cheese is melted. Let stand 10 minutes before serving. Cut into wedges. Sprinkle with parsley.

1 Serving: Calories 470; Total Fat 26g (Saturated Fat 15g; Trans Fat 1g); Cholesterol 150mg; Sodium 1050mg; Total Carbohydrate 30g (Dietary Fiber 1g); Protein 28g **Exchanges:** ½ Other Carbohydrate, 2 Low-Fat Milk, 1½ Lean Meat, 2½ Fat **Carbohydrate Choices:** 2

Primavera Pie

Prep Time: 20 Minutes • **Start to Finish:** 1 Hour 25 Minutes • 8 servings

2½ cups Original Bisquick® mix

6 tablespoons cold butter

¼ cup boiling water

1 cup grated Parmesan cheese

8 oz fresh asparagus, trimmed, cut into 1½-inch pieces

¾ cup chopped roasted red bell peppers (from a jar)

2 teaspoons chopped fresh oregano leaves

1 tablespoon vegetable oil

1 medium zucchini, sliced

1 medium yellow squash, sliced

1 cup half-and-half

½ teaspoon salt

½ teaspoon freshly ground pepper

4 eggs

2 tablespoons bread crumbs

1 Heat oven to 350°F. Spray 9½-inch glass deep-dish pie plate with cooking spray.

2 In medium bowl, place Bisquick mix. Cut in butter, using pastry blender or fork, until mixture looks like coarse crumbs. Add boiling water; stir vigorously until soft dough forms. With fingers dipped in Bisquick mix, press dough in bottom and up side of pie plate, forming edge on rim of plate.

3 Sprinkle ½ cup of the cheese over bottom of crust. Arrange asparagus in even layer over cheese; top with roasted peppers and oregano.

4 In 12-inch skillet, heat oil over medium-high heat. Add zucchini and yellow squash; cook 2 minutes or just until tender. Layer over mixture in pie plate, overlapping slightly.

5 In medium bowl, beat half-and-half, salt, pepper and eggs with whisk. Pour over vegetables. Sprinkle with remaining ½ cup cheese and the bread crumbs.

6 Bake 45 to 50 minutes or until knife inserted in center comes out clean. Let stand 15 minutes before serving. Cut into wedges.

1 Serving: Calories 400; Total Fat 25g (Saturated Fat 12g; Trans Fat 0g); Cholesterol 0mg; Sodium 1018mg; Total Carbohydrate 31g (Dietary Fiber 2g); Protein 14g **Exchanges:** 2 Starch, ½ Vegetable, 1½ Medium-Fat Meat, 3½ Fat **Carbohydrate Choices:** 2

Impossibly Easy Mexicali Chicken Pie

Prep Time: 20 Minutes • **Start to Finish:** 50 Minutes • 6 servings

1 cup chopped or shredded cooked chicken

1 cup frozen whole kernel corn

1 can (2¼ oz) sliced ripe olives, drained

1 small onion, chopped (⅓ cup)

1 tablespoon chopped green chiles (from 4.5-oz can)

2 cups shredded Monterey Jack cheese (8 oz)

½ cup Original Bisquick® mix

1 cup milk

2 eggs

½ teaspoon salt

¼ teaspoon pepper

½ cup sour cream

½ cup guacamole

1 cup chunky-style salsa

1 Heat oven to 400°F. Spray 9-inch glass pie plate or 8-inch square (2-quart) glass baking dish with cooking spray.

2 In large bowl, mix chicken, corn, olives, onion, chiles and cheese. Spoon mixture into pie plate.

3 In medium bowl, stir Bisquick mix, milk, eggs, salt and pepper with whisk until blended. Pour batter evenly over chicken mixture.

4 Bake 28 to 30 minutes or until knife inserted in center comes out clean. Let stand 5 minutes before serving. Cut into wedges. Top with sour cream, guacamole and salsa.

1 Serving: Calories 380; Total Fat 23g (Saturated Fat 12g; Trans Fat 1g); Cholesterol 135mg; Sodium 1080mg; Total Carbohydrate 20g (Dietary Fiber 2g); Protein 21g
Exchanges: ½ Starch, ½ Other Carbohydrate, ½ Vegetable, 2½ Medium-Fat Meat, 2 Fat
Carbohydrate Choices: 1

Impossibly Easy Mexicali Chicken Pie developed by Jackie Colwell of Oregon City, OR, won honorable mention in our Better with Bisquick Contest.

Impossibly Easy Buffalo Chicken Pie

Prep Time: 20 Minutes • **Start to Finish:** 1 Hour • 6 servings

¼ cup blue cheese dressing

¼ cup red pepper sauce

1 package (3 oz) cream cheese, softened

1¼ cups cubed cooked chicken

½ cup chopped celery

¼ cup sliced green onions (4 medium)

1 cup shredded Swiss cheese (4 oz)

¾ cup Original Bisquick® mix

½ teaspoon salt

¼ teaspoon pepper

¾ cup milk

3 eggs

Additional blue cheese dressing, if desired

1 Heat oven to 400°F. Spray 9-inch glass pie plate with cooking spray.

2 In small bowl, stir dressing, pepper sauce and cream cheese until blended. Spread in bottom of pie plate. Top with chicken, celery, green onions and Swiss cheese.

3 In medium bowl, stir remaining ingredients with whisk or fork until blended. Pour batter over ingredients in pie plate.

4 Bake 25 to 30 minutes or until top is golden brown and center is set. Let stand 10 minutes before serving. Cut into wedges. Serve with additional dressing.

1 Serving: Calories 350; Total Fat 23g (Saturated Fat 9g; Trans Fat 1g); Cholesterol 170mg; Sodium 920mg; Total Carbohydrate 17g (Dietary Fiber 1g); Protein 19g **Exchanges:** ½ Starch, ½ Low-Fat Milk, 2 Lean Meat, 3 Fat **Carbohydrate Choices:** 1

> Change the flavor a bit by substituting ranch dressing for the blue cheese dressing or Cheddar cheese for the Swiss cheese.

Gluten-Free Hearty Chicken Pot Pie

Prep Time: 15 Minutes • **Start to Finish:** 45 Minutes • 6 servings

2 tablespoons butter

1 medium onion, chopped (½ cup)

1 bag (12 oz) frozen mixed vegetables

1½ cups cut-up cooked chicken

1¾ cups gluten-free chicken broth (from 32-oz carton)

1 teaspoon gluten-free seasoned salt

½ teaspoon dried thyme leaves

1¼ cups milk

3 tablespoons cornstarch

¾ cup Bisquick® Gluten Free mix

1 egg

2 tablespoons butter, melted

1 tablespoon chopped fresh parsley

1 Heat oven to 350°F. In 3-quart saucepan, melt 2 tablespoons butter over medium heat. Cook onion in butter, stirring frequently, until tender. Stir in vegetables, chicken, broth, seasoned salt and thyme; heat to boiling.

2 In small bowl, mix ¾ cup of the milk and the cornstarch with whisk until smooth; stir into chicken mixture. Heat just to boiling. Pour into ungreased 11x7-inch (2-quart) glass baking dish.

3 In small bowl, stir Bisquick mix, egg, melted butter and remaining ½ cup milk with fork until blended. Drop mixture by small spoonfuls over chicken mixture. Sprinkle with parsley.

4 Bake 25 to 30 minutes or until toothpick inserted in center of topping comes out clean.

1 Serving: Calories 280; Total Fat 13g (Saturated Fat 6g; Trans Fat 0g); Cholesterol 0mg; Sodium 860mg; Total Carbohydrate 25g (Dietary Fiber 2g); Protein 15g **Exchanges:** 1 Starch, ½ Other Carbohydrate, 2 Medium-Fat Meat, ½ Fat **Carbohydrate Choices:** 1½

If you are cooking gluten free, always read labels to make sure each recipe ingredient is gluten free. Products and ingredient sources can change.

Impossibly Easy Mini Thai Chicken Pies

Prep Time: 20 Minutes • **Start to Finish:** 1 Hour 15 Minutes • 6 servings (2 mini pies each)

CHICKEN MIXTURE

- 1 tablespoon vegetable oil
- 1 lb boneless skinless chicken breasts, cut into bite-size pieces
- 1 medium onion, chopped (½ cup)
- ¼ cup sliced green onions (4 medium)
- ¼ cup fresh cilantro, chopped
- ½ teaspoon Thai red curry paste
- 1 tablespoon fresh lime juice
- 1 cup shredded mozzarella cheese (4 oz)

BAKING MIXTURE

- ½ cup Original Bisquick® mix
- ½ cup milk
- 2 eggs

GARNISHES

- ½ cup salted cocktail peanuts
- ¼ cup sliced green onions (4 medium)

1 Heat oven to 375°F. Spray 12 regular-size muffin cups with cooking spray.

2 In 10-inch nonstick skillet, heat oil over medium-high heat. Add chicken; cook 5 to 7 minutes, stirring occasionally, until chicken is no longer pink in center. Add chopped onion; cook 2 to 3 minutes. Add green onions, cilantro, curry paste and lime juice, stirring occasionally, until mixture is thoroughly heated. Remove from heat. Cool 5 minutes; stir in cheese.

3 In medium bowl, stir remaining ingredients with whisk or fork until blended. Spoon about 1 tablespoon baking mixture into each muffin cup. Top each with ¼ cup chicken mixture and 1 tablespoon baking mixture.

4 Bake 10 minutes. Carefully open oven and sprinkle about 1 table-spoon peanuts on top of each muffin. Bake 20 to 25 minutes longer or until toothpick inserted in center comes out clean and tops of pies are golden brown. Cool 5 minutes. With thin knife, loosen sides of muffins from pan. Remove pies from pan to cooling rack. Cool 10 minutes. Garnish with green onions.

1 Serving: Calories 330; Total Fat 18g (Saturated Fat 5g; Trans Fat 0.5g); Cholesterol 120mg; Sodium 430mg; Total Carbohydrate 13g (Dietary Fiber 1g); Protein 28g **Exchanges:** 1 Starch, 3 Very Lean Meat, 2½ Fat **Carbohydrate Choices:** 1

Make It Your Way Impossibly Easy Pies

WHAT ARE IMPOSSIBLY EASY PIES?

Unlike regular pies that require a crust to be made separate from the filling, Impossibly Easy Pies magically form their own crust as they bake. Simply mix the ingredients together and pour or layer them in a pie plate. Some of the Bisquick batter sinks to the bottom and a wonderful crust-like layer is formed. A delicious filling, similar to a quiche or custard, bakes over this layer, creating the classic Impossibly Easy Pie. You can make full-size Impossibly Easy Pies for breakfast, brunch, dinner and dessert. Mini versions can be made and are ideal for meals or appetizers.

Impossibly Easy Pies are easily doubled for larger groups. Just double all of the ingredients and bake in two 9-inch pie plates or one 13x9-inch (3-quart) glass baking dish. For the 13x9-inch dish, the bake time may need to increase slightly to be sure that the center is done.

GET A JUMP START

Impossibly Easy Pies are best prepared just before baking. Get a head start on dinner by prepping the solid ingredients the night before, placing them right in the pie plate. Cover the pie plate and refrigerate until you're ready to finish and bake the pie. The next night, whip up the Bisquick batter portion of the recipe, pour it over the ingredients in the pie plate and pop the pie in the oven.

STORING AND REHEATING

If you are lucky enough to have any remaining cooked pie, cover and store it in the refrigerator up to 3 days. It makes a great quick breakfast or easy, hot, homemade lunch. To reheat a slice, place it on a microwavable plate and cover with waxed paper. Microwave on Medium (50%) for 2 to 3 minutes or until hot.

GLUTEN-FREE OR HEART-SMART PIES

Gluten-Free and Heart-Smart Bisquick have different formulations and may work differently than Original Bisquick® in recipes, so you won't want to make any substitution of products. For the best results, follow Impossibly Easy Pie recipes designed for these products.

MAKE IT YOUR WAY—CUSTOMIZE YOUR PIES

Have some leftover ingredients you'd like to use up lurking in your refrigerator? Use our Impossibly Easy Cheeseburger Pie (page 238) as the base recipe for your own creation. Use whatever you have on hand or what you're in the mood for, to make your own flavor of pie. Follow these easy tricks and dinner will be on the table in no time:

- Substitute 1 pound of any uncooked ground meat for the ground beef—chicken, turkey, bulk Italian sausage, chorizo or pork are all good choices.

- Substitute 1¼–1½ cups cut-up cooked meat (such as chicken, turkey or pork) for the ground beef. Spray the skillet with cooking spray and cook the onion and salt before adding cooked meat.

- Change the vegetables: Omit the onion and add about 1 cup cooked or about 9 to 10 ounces frozen, thawed vegetables to the cooked ground beef in the pie plate. You may need to add a few minutes of extra bake time to ensure the vegetables are tender.

- Swap the cheese: use any flavor of shredded cheese you would like, in place of the Cheddar.

Italian Artichoke Bacon Pie

Prep Time: 15 Minutes • **Start to Finish:** 50 Minutes • 6 servings

1 cup shredded mozzarella cheese (4 oz)

12 slices bacon, crisply cooked, crumbled (¾ cup)

¼ cup chopped sun-dried tomatoes in olive oil, drained

¼ cup creamy Italian dressing

1 jar (6 oz) marinated artichoke hearts, drained, chopped

½ cup Original Bisquick® mix

¼ cup grated Parmesan cheese

½ teaspoon garlic powder

1 cup milk

2 eggs

1 Heat oven to 400°F. Spray 9-inch glass pie plate with cooking spray.

2 In large bowl, mix mozzarella cheese, bacon, sun-dried tomatoes, dressing and artichokes. Spread mixture in pie plate.

3 In medium bowl, beat remaining ingredients with whisk or fork until blended. Pour batter over mixture in pie plate.

4 Bake 25 to 30 minutes or until golden brown and knife inserted in center comes out clean. Let stand 5 minutes before serving. Cut into wedges.

1 Serving: Calories 280; Total Fat 17g (Saturated Fat 6g; Trans Fat 0.5g); Cholesterol 100mg; Sodium 820mg; Total Carbohydrate 16g (Dietary Fiber 3g); Protein 15g **Exchanges:** ½ Starch, ½ Other Carbohydrate, 2 Medium-Fat Meat, 1 Fat **Carbohydrate Choices:** 1

Garnish this Italian pie with olives and pepperoncini peppers or giardiniera vegetable mix.

Try 4 ounces crumbled feta cheese instead of the mozzarella cheese.

Peppered Bacon Hash Brown Pie

Prep Time: 25 Minutes • **Start to Finish:** 2 Hours • 8 servings

BACON

3 tablespoons brown sugar

1½ teaspoons coarse ground black pepper

12 slices center-cut bacon

CRUST

2½ cups Original Bisquick® mix

6 tablespoons cold butter

¼ cup boiling water

FILLING

1 cup frozen diced hash brown potatoes, thawed

1½ cups shredded sharp Cheddar cheese (6 oz)

4 green onions, sliced (¼ cup)

1½ cups half-and-half

4 eggs

½ teaspoon salt

1 cup grape tomatoes, halved

1 Heat oven to 425°F. Line 15x10x1-inch pan with foil; place wire cooling rack in pan.

2 In small bowl, mix brown sugar and pepper. Sprinkle over 1 side of each bacon slice, pressing firmly. Place bacon on rack.

3 Bake 18 to 20 minutes or until crisp. Reduce oven temperature to 350°F. Spray 9½-inch glass deep-dish pie plate with cooking spray.

4 In large bowl, place Bisquick mix. Cut in butter, using pastry blender or fork, until mixture looks like coarse crumbs. Add boiling water; stir vigorously until soft dough forms. With fingers dipped in Bisquick mix, press dough in bottom and up side of pie plate, forming edge on rim of plate.

5 Crumble 8 slices of the bacon. Sprinkle crumbled bacon, potatoes, cheese and onions over crust. In medium bowl, beat half-and-half, eggs and salt with whisk until blended. Pour batter over ingredients in crust.

6 Bake 50 to 55 minutes or until knife inserted in center comes out clean. Let stand 10 minutes before serving. Cut into 8 wedges. Cut remaining 4 slices of the bacon in half. Top each wedge with half slice of bacon and 2 tablespoons tomatoes.

1 Serving: Calories 500; Total Fat 32g (Saturated Fat 17g; Trans Fat 0g); Cholesterol 0mg; Sodium 1118mg; Total Carbohydrate 39g (Dietary Fiber 2g); Protein 16g **Exchanges:** 2 Starch, ½ Other Carbohydrate, ½ Medium-Fat Meat, 1 High-Fat Meat, 4 Fat **Carbohydrate Choices:** 2½

Impossibly Easy Ham and Swiss Pie

Prep Time: 10 Minutes • **Start to Finish:** 55 Minutes • 6 servings

1½ cups cubed fully cooked smoked boneless ham

1 cup shredded Swiss cheese (4 oz)

¼ cup chopped green onions or chopped onion

½ cup Original Bisquick® mix

1 cup milk

¼ teaspoon salt, if desired

⅛ teaspoon pepper

2 eggs

1 medium tomato, chopped

1 medium green bell pepper, chopped

1 Heat oven to 400°F. Grease 9-inch glass pie plate with shortening or cooking spray.

2 Sprinkle ham, cheese and onions in pie plate.

3 In medium bowl, stir Bisquick mix, milk, salt, pepper and eggs until blended. Pour batter over mixture in pie plate.

4 Bake 35 to 40 minutes or until knife inserted in center comes out clean. Let stand 5 minutes before serving. Cut into wedges. Garnish with tomato and bell pepper.

1 Serving: Calories 230; Total Fat 12g (Saturated Fat 6g; Trans Fat 0.5g); Cholesterol 110mg; Sodium 700mg; Total Carbohydrate 12g (Dietary Fiber 0g); Protein 17g
Exchanges: ½ Starch, ½ Other Carbohydrate, 2 Lean Meat, 1 Fat **Carbohydrate Choices:** 1

This pie can be covered and refrigerated up to 24 hours before baking. You may need to bake a bit longer than the recipe directs since you'll be starting with a cold pie. Watch carefully for doneness.

Impossibly Easy Cheeseburger Pie

Prep Time: 15 Minutes • **Start to Finish:** 40 Minutes • 6 servings

1 lb lean (at least 80%) ground beef

1 large onion, chopped (1 cup)

½ teaspoon salt

1 cup shredded Cheddar cheese (4 oz)

½ cup Original Bisquick® mix

1 cup milk

2 eggs

1 Heat oven to 400°F. Spray 9-inch glass pie plate with cooking spray.

2 In 10-inch skillet, cook beef and onion over medium heat 8 to 10 minutes, stirring occasionally, until beef is browned; drain. Stir in salt. Spread in pie plate. Sprinkle with cheese.

3 In small bowl, stir remaining ingredients with fork or whisk until blended. Pour batter over ingredients in pie plate.

4 Bake 23 to 25 minutes or until knife inserted in center comes out clean. Let stand 5 minutes before serving. Cut into wedges.

1 Serving: Calories 300; Total Fat 19g (Saturated Fat 9g; Trans Fat 1g); Cholesterol 130mg; Sodium 510mg; Total Carbohydrate 11g (Dietary Fiber 0g); Protein 22g **Exchanges:** 1 Other Carbohydrate, 2½ Lean Meat, ½ High-Fat Meat, 1½ Fat **Carbohydrate Choices:** 1

> Top off this delicious pie just like you would a cheeseburger. Serve with barbecue sauce, bacon, ketchup, salsa and sliced tomato. Or try pineapple slices or avocado if you like.
>
> This pie can be covered and refrigerated up to 24 hours before baking. You may need to bake a bit longer than the recipe directs since you'll be starting with a cold pie. Watch carefully for doneness.

Impossibly Easy Beef, Broccoli and Mushroom Pie

Prep Time: 15 Minutes • **Start to Finish:** 35 Minutes • **6 servings**

1 lb chopped cooked roast beef (about 2 cups)

¼ cup chopped green onions

1 box (9 oz) frozen cut broccoli, thawed

1 jar (4 oz) sliced mushrooms, drained

½ cup Original Bisquick® mix

1 cup milk

¼ cup sour cream

2 eggs

½ teaspoon salt

½ teaspoon pepper

½ cup shredded Swiss cheese

Fresh parsley sprigs, if desired

1 Heat oven to 400°F. Grease 9-inch glass pie plate with shortening or cooking spray.

2 In medium bowl, mix beef, onions, broccoli and mushrooms; spoon into pie plate.

3 In same bowl, stir Bisquick mix, milk, sour cream, eggs, salt and pepper until blended. Pour batter over beef mixture in pie plate. Top with cheese.

4 Bake 30 to 35 minutes or until knife inserted in center comes out clean. Let stand 5 minutes before serving. Cut into wedges. Garnish with parsley.

1 Serving: Calories 300; Total Fat 12g (Saturated Fat 5g; Trans Fat 0.5g); Cholesterol 155mg; Sodium 460mg; Total Carbohydrate 12g (Dietary Fiber 2g); Protein 35g
Exchanges: ½ Starch, ½ Vegetable, 4½ Lean Meat **Carbohydrate Choices:** 1

This pie can be covered and refrigerated up to 24 hours before baking. You may need to bake a bit longer than the recipe directs since you'll be starting with a cold pie. Watch carefully for doneness.

Chicken Chile Cobbler

Prep Time: 30 Minutes • **Start to Finish:** 1 Hour 10 Minutes • 10 servings

FILLING

- 1 bag (16 oz) frozen black-eyed peas
- 2 tablespoons butter
- 1 lb smoked sausage, cut into ¼-inch slices
- 1 large sweet onion, finely chopped
- 1 large poblano chile, seeded, diced
- ¼ cup all-purpose flour
- 1 package (1.25 oz) white chicken chili seasoning mix
- 3 cups chicken broth (from 32-oz carton)
- 3 cups chopped cooked chicken

CRUST

- 1 package (8.5 oz) microwavable long-grain and wild rice mix
- 1 cup Original Bisquick® mix
- ¾ cup milk
- 1 egg, slightly beaten

1 Heat oven to 425°F. Cook black-eyed peas as directed on package; drain.

2 In 4-quart ovenproof Dutch oven or saucepan, melt butter over medium-high heat; cook sausage in butter 3 minutes or until lightly browned. Add onion and poblano chile; cook 3 minutes. Stir in flour and seasoning mix; cook and stir 1 minute. Gradually add broth, stirring to loosen particles from bottom of Dutch oven. Cook 3 minutes, stirring constantly, until broth begins to thicken. Stir in peas and chicken; heat to boiling.

3 In large bowl, mix rice and Bisquick mix. Stir in milk and egg just until moistened. Immediately spoon batter over hot chicken mixture in Dutch oven.

4 Bake 35 to 40 minutes or until crust is cooked through and golden brown.

1 Serving: Calories 434; Total Fat 20g (Saturated Fat 7g; Trans Fat 0g); Cholesterol 0mg; Sodium 1184mg; Total Carbohydrate 34g (Dietary Fiber 4g); Protein 27g **Exchanges:** 2 Starch, 1½ Lean Meat, 1½ High-Fat Meat, ½ Fat **Carbohydrate Choices:** 2

Sausage, Spinach and Cheese Tart

Prep Time: 20 Minutes • **Start to Finish:** 1 Hour 25 Minutes • **6 servings**

1 can (15 to 16 oz) cannellini beans, drained, rinsed

1⅓ cups Original Bisquick® mix

⅓ cup Italian dressing

½ lb bulk Italian sausage

1 box (9 oz) frozen chopped spinach, thawed, squeezed to drain*

1 can (14.5 oz) diced tomatoes, drained

1 tablespoon dried oregano leaves

1¼ cups shredded mozzarella cheese (5 oz)

6 eggs

1 cup milk

½ cup whipping cream

1 Heat oven to 375°F. Grease 9-inch springform pan with shortening or cooking spray.

2 In medium bowl, mash beans with potato masher or fork until almost smooth. Stir in Bisquick mix and dressing. Spread mixture in bottom and up side of springform pan.

3 Bake 10 to 12 minutes or until set.

4 Meanwhile, in 10-inch skillet, cook sausage over medium-high heat 7 to 9 minutes or until no longer pink; drain. Remove from heat. Stir in spinach, tomatoes, oregano and 1 cup of the cheese until well blended. Spoon mixture over prebaked crust.

5 In medium bowl, beat eggs, milk and cream with whisk until well blended. Pour over sausage mixture.

6 Bake 30 minutes. Sprinkle with remaining ¼ cup cheese. Bake 20 to 25 minutes longer or until top is golden brown, center is firm and knife inserted in center comes out clean. Let stand 10 minutes. Loosen edge of tart from side of pan; remove side of pan. Cut into wedges.

*To quickly thaw spinach, cut a small slit in the center of the pouch; microwave on High 2 to 3 minutes or until thawed. Remove spinach from the pouch; squeeze dry with paper towels.

1 Serving: Calories 540; Total Fat 28g (Saturated Fat 11g; Trans Fat 1g); Cholesterol 230mg; Sodium 850mg; Total Carbohydrate 47g (Dietary Fiber 7g); Protein 27g **Exchanges:** 2 Starch, 1 Low-Fat Milk, 1 Vegetable, 1½ Medium-Fat Meat, 3 Fat **Carbohydrate Choices:** 3

Sausage, Spinach and Cheese Tart is a 2013 Bisquick Family Favorites Recipe Contest award-winning recipe developed by Steve Beeson, 3rd Place, Wisconsin State Fair (Milwaukee, WI).

Tomato Tart

Prep Time: 20 Minutes • **Start to Finish:** 1 Hour 40 Minutes • **10 servings**

- 1 lb assorted tomatoes, cut into ½-inch slices
- ½ teaspoon salt
- ½ cup butter, softened
- 2 cups Original Bisquick® mix
- 3 tablespoons boiling water
- 1 cup shredded mozzarella cheese (4 oz)
- ½ cup shredded Parmesan cheese (2 oz)
- ½ cup sandwich spread, mayonnaise or salad dressing
- 3 medium green onions, chopped (3 tablespoons)
- 1 tablespoon chopped fresh basil
- ¼ teaspoon freshly ground pepper

1 Place tomato slices in single layer on paper towels; sprinkle with salt. Let stand 30 minutes.

2 Meanwhile, heat oven to 400°F. Spray 9-inch tart pan with removable bottom with cooking spray.

3 In medium bowl, place Bisquick mix. Cut in butter, using pastry blender or fork, until mixture looks like coarse crumbs. Add boiling water; stir vigorously until soft dough forms. With fingers dipped in Bisquick mix, press dough in bottom and up side of tart pan. Freeze 10 minutes.

4 Bake 14 to 15 minutes or until light golden brown. Sprinkle partially baked crust with ½ cup of the mozzarella cheese. Cool 10 minutes in pan on cooling rack. Reduce oven temperature to 350°F.

5 In medium bowl, mix remaining ½ cup mozzarella cheese, the Parmesan cheese, sandwich spread, green onions and basil. Spread over cheese and crust. Pat tomatoes dry with paper towels; arrange over cheese mixture. Sprinkle with pepper.

6 Bake 30 to 35 minutes or until crust is golden brown. Let stand 10 minutes. Remove tart from side of pan. Garnish with additional chopped basil. Cut into wedges.

1 Serving: Calories 420; Total Fat 32g (Saturated Fat 13g; Trans Fat 0g); Cholesterol 0mg; Sodium 930mg; Total Carbohydrate 25g (Dietary Fiber 1g); Protein 10g **Exchanges:** 1½ Starch, ½ Vegetable, ½ Medium-Fat Meat, 5½ Fat **Carbohydrate Choices:** 1½

Bacon and Greens Quiche

Prep Time: 20 Minutes • **Start to Finish:** 1 Hour 15 Minutes • **8 servings**

1¼ cups Original Bisquick® mix

3 tablespoons butter, softened

2 tablespoons boiling water

4 slices thick-sliced bacon

3 cups coarsely chopped turnip greens

½ cup chopped red bell pepper

⅓ cup sliced green onions (5 to 6 medium)

1 cup shredded pepper Jack cheese (4 oz)

4 eggs

1½ cups half-and-half

¼ teaspoon salt

¼ teaspoon freshly ground pepper

1 Heat oven to 350°F. Spray 9-inch glass pie plate with cooking spray.

2 In medium bowl, stir Bisquick mix and butter until blended. Add boiling water; stir vigorously until soft dough forms. With fingers dipped in Bisquick mix, press dough in bottom and up side of pie plate, forming edge on rim of plate.

3 In 10-inch skillet, cook bacon until crisp; drain on paper towels. Reserve 2 tablespoons drippings in skillet. Crumble bacon; set aside. Cook turnip greens and bell pepper in drippings over medium heat 3 to 4 minutes, stirring occasionally, just until tender. Stir in green onions; spoon mixture into pie plate. Sprinkle with cheese and crumbled bacon.

4 In large bowl, mix eggs, half-and-half, salt and pepper with fork or whisk until blended. Pour over greens mixture in crust.

5 Bake 40 to 45 minutes or until knife inserted in center comes out clean. Let stand 10 minutes before serving. Cut into wedges.

1 Serving: Calories 288; Total Fat 20g (Saturated Fat 11g; Trans Fat 0g); Cholesterol 0mg; Sodium 554mg; Total Carbohydrate 17g (Dietary Fiber 2g); Protein 10g **Exchanges:** 1 Starch, ½ Vegetable, ½ Medium-Fat Meat, ½ High-Fat Meat, 2½ Fat **Carbohydrate Choices:** 1

Ham, Pineapple and Cheddar Quiche

Prep Time: 20 Minutes • **Start to Finish:** 1 Hour 15 Minutes • **6 servings**

CRUST

1¼ cups Original Bisquick® mix

3 tablespoons cold butter

2 tablespoons boiling water

FILLING

1½ cups shredded sharp Cheddar cheese (6 oz)

¾ cup finely chopped cooked ham (4 oz)

3 medium green onions, sliced (3 tablespoons)

1 can (8 oz) pineapple tidbits in juice, well drained

3 eggs

¾ cup half-and-half

¼ teaspoon white pepper

GARNISH, IF DESIRED

Additional sliced green onions

1 Heat oven to 350°F. Spray 9-inch glass pie plate with cooking spray.

2 In medium bowl, place Bisquick mix. Cut in butter, using pastry blender or fork, until mixture looks like coarse crumbs. Add boiling water; stir vigorously until soft dough forms. With fingers dipped in Bisquick mix, press dough in bottom and up side of pie plate, forming edge on rim of plate.

3 Sprinkle cheese, ham, 3 tablespoons onions and the pineapple in crust. In medium bowl, beat eggs, half-and-half and pepper until blended. Pour over ingredients in crust.

4 Bake 40 to 45 minutes or until knife inserted in center comes out clean. Let stand 10 minutes before serving. Garnish with additional onions. Cut into wedges.

1 Serving: Calories 390; Total Fat 26g (Saturated Fat 14g; Trans Fat 1.5g); Cholesterol 175mg; Sodium 850mg; Total Carbohydrate 22g (Dietary Fiber 1g); Protein 18g **Exchanges:** 1 Starch, ½ Other Carbohydrate, 2 Medium-Fat Meat, 3 Fat **Carbohydrate Choices:** 1½

Shrimp and Artichoke Quiche

Prep Time: 10 Minutes • **Start to Finish:** 55 Minutes • 6 servings

¾ **lb frozen cooked deveined peeled shrimp, thawed, tail shells removed, coarsely chopped (1½ cups)**

3 **medium green onions, sliced (3 tablespoons)**

1 **cup shredded Swiss cheese (4 oz)**

1 **cup shredded Parmesan cheese (4 oz)**

1 **cup Original Bisquick® mix**

2 **eggs**

1 **cup milk**

1½ **teaspoons Cajun seasoning**

1 **can (14 oz) artichoke hearts, drained, cut lengthwise in half**

1 Heat oven to 400°F. Lightly spray 9-inch glass pie plate with cooking spray. Sprinkle shrimp and onions in pie plate.

2 In small bowl, mix cheeses. Sprinkle 1 cup of the cheese mixture over shrimp and onions.

3 In medium bowl, stir Bisquick mix, eggs, milk and Cajun seasoning with fork or whisk until blended. Pour evenly over cheeses. Top with artichoke heart halves, cut side down, and remaining 1 cup cheese mixture.

4 Bake 30 to 35 minutes or until knife inserted in center comes out clean. Let stand 10 minutes before serving. Cut into wedges.

1 Serving: Calories 363; Total Fat 17g (Saturated Fat 9g; Trans Fat 0g); Cholesterol 0mg; Sodium 1425mg; Total Carbohydrate 20g (Dietary Fiber 1g); Protein 31g **Exchanges:** 1 Starch, 1 Vegetable, 3 Very Lean Meat, 1 High-Fat Meat, 1 Fat **Carbohydrate Choices:** 1½

Chiles Rellenos Quiche

Prep Time: 10 Minutes • **Start to Finish:** 1 Hour 5 Minutes • 6 servings

2 cans (4.5 oz each) chopped green chiles, drained

2 cups shredded sharp Cheddar cheese (8 oz)

1 cup shredded pepper Jack cheese (4 oz)

2 cups milk

1 cup Original Bisquick® mix

4 eggs, slightly beaten

1 cup ricotta cheese

Pico de gallo or fresh salsa, if desired

Fresh cilantro leaves, if desired

1 Heat oven to 350°F. Spray 11x7-inch (2-quart) glass baking dish with cooking spray.

2 Sprinkle chiles, Cheddar cheese and pepper Jack cheese evenly into baking dish. In large bowl, beat milk, Bisquick mix and eggs with electric mixer on low speed until smooth. Stir in ricotta cheese. Spoon batter evenly over ingredients in baking dish.

3 Bake 45 minutes or until knife inserted in center comes out clean. Let stand 10 minutes before serving. Cut into squares. Garnish with pico de gallo and cilantro.

1 Serving: Calories 479; Total Fat 31g (Saturated Fat 17g; Trans Fat 0g); Cholesterol 0mg; Sodium 968mg; Total Carbohydrate 20g (Dietary Fiber 1g); Protein 26g **Exchanges:** 1 Starch, ½ Other Carbohydrate, 3 High-Fat Meat **Carbohydrate Choices:** 1½

Three-Cheese Spinach and Pasta Bake

Prep Time: 30 Minutes • **Start to Finish:** 1 Hour 15 Minutes • 10 servings

1 **package (8 oz) sliced fresh mushrooms (about 3 cups)**

¼ **cup finely chopped onion**

1 **package (7 oz) small pasta shells (2 cups), cooked, drained**

2 **boxes (9 oz each) frozen chopped spinach, thawed, squeezed to drain***

1 **cup Original Bisquick® mix**

1 **cup shredded mozzarella cheese (4 oz)**

⅓ **cup grated Parmesan cheese**

1 **teaspoon salt**

½ **teaspoon pepper**

1¾ **cups milk**

1 **package (4 oz) crumbled tomato-basil feta cheese (1 cup)**

1 Heat oven to 375°F. Spray 13x9-inch (3-quart) glass baking dish with cooking spray.

2 In 8-inch nonstick skillet, cook mushrooms and onion over medium heat about 5 minutes, stirring frequently, until tender.

3 In large bowl, mix pasta and spinach. Stir in mushroom mixture. Spread in baking dish.

4 In large bowl, stir remaining ingredients until blended. Pour over spinach mixture.

5 Bake 35 to 40 minutes or until top is golden brown. Let stand 5 minutes before serving. Cut into squares.

*To quickly thaw spinach, cut a small slit in the center of the pouch; microwave on High 2 to 3 minutes or until thawed. Remove spinach from the pouch; squeeze dry with paper towels.

1 Serving: Calories 200; Total Fat 9g (Saturated Fat 5g; Trans Fat 0.5g); Cholesterol 25mg; Sodium 700mg; Total Carbohydrate 20g (Dietary Fiber 2g); Protein 11g **Exchanges:** 1 Starch, ½ Low-Fat Milk, ½ Vegetable, 1 Fat **Carbohydrate Choices:** 1

Easy Baked Chicken and Potato Dinner

Prep Time: 20 Minutes • **Start to Finish:** 1 Hour • **2 servings**

½ cup Bisquick Heart Smart® mix

2 boneless skinless chicken breasts

2 tablespoons Dijon mustard

¾ lb small red potatoes, cut into quarters

1 small red or green bell pepper, cut into ½-inch pieces

1 small onion, cut into 8 wedges

Cooking spray

2 tablespoons grated Parmesan cheese, if desired

½ teaspoon paprika

1 Heat oven to 400°F. Spray 13x9-inch (3-quart) glass baking dish with cooking spray.

2 In shallow dish, place Bisquick mix. Brush chicken with 1 table-spoon of the mustard; then coat with Bisquick mix. Place chicken breasts in baking dish at opposite ends. Place potatoes, bell pepper and onion in center of dish; brush vegetables with remaining mustard. Spray chicken and vegetables with cooking spray; sprinkle evenly with cheese and paprika.

3 Bake 35 to 40 minutes, stirring vegetables after 20 minutes, until potatoes are tender and juice of chicken is clear when center of thickest part is cut (at least 165°F).

1 Serving: Calories 430; Total Fat 8g (Saturated Fat 1.5g; Trans Fat 0g); Cholesterol 75mg; Sodium 770mg; Total Carbohydrate 58g (Dietary Fiber 6g); Protein 33g **Exchanges:** 2½ Starch, 1 Other Carbohydrate, 1 Vegetable, 3 Very Lean Meat, 1 Fat **Carbohydrate Choices:** 4

> **Try different varieties of potatoes for color and flavor. Choose Yukon gold, purple, yellow Finnish or Texas finger potatoes.**

Oven-Fried Pork Cutlets with Apple Slaw

Prep Time: 10 Minutes • **Start to Finish:** 30 Minutes • 4 servings

CUTLETS

- 4 boneless pork loin chops, ½ inch thick (about 1 lb)
- 8 saltine crackers, finely crushed (⅓ cup)
- ½ cup Original Bisquick® mix
- ½ teaspoon paprika
- ¼ teaspoon pepper
- 1 egg or ¼ cup fat-free egg product
- 1 tablespoon water
  Cooking spray

SLAW

- 4 cups coleslaw mix (shredded cabbage and carrots)
- 1 small tart red apple, coarsely chopped (1 cup)
- ¼ cup chopped onion
- ⅓ cup fat-free coleslaw dressing
- ⅛ teaspoon celery seed

1 Heat oven to 425°F. Generously spray 15x10x1-inch pan with cooking spray.

2 Between pieces of plastic wrap or waxed paper, place each pork chop; gently pound with flat side of meat mallet or rolling pin until about ¼ inch thick.

3 In small shallow dish, mix crackers, Bisquick mix, paprika and pepper. In another shallow dish, beat egg and water. Dip pork chops into egg, then coat with cracker mixture. Repeat dipping coated pork in egg and in cracker mixture. Place in pan. Generously spray tops of pork chops with cooking spray.

4 Bake about 18 to 22 minutes or until pork chops are golden brown and meat thermometer inserted in center reads 145°F.

5 Meanwhile, in large bowl, toss all slaw ingredients. Serve slaw with pork cutlets.

1 Serving: Calories 360; Total Fat 14g (Saturated Fat 4.5g; Trans Fat 1g); Cholesterol 125mg; Sodium 480mg; Total Carbohydrate 29g (Dietary Fiber 3g); Protein 29g
Exchanges: ½ Starch, 1 Other Carbohydrate, 1 Vegetable, 3½ Lean Meat, 1 Fat
Carbohydrate Choices: 2

> Substitute thinly shredded red cabbage for the coleslaw mix. For 4 cups shredded cabbage, you'll need about a 1-pound medium head of red cabbage.

Fish with Tomato-Bacon-Avocado Salsa

Prep Time: 25 Minutes • **Start to Finish: 45 Minutes** • **6 servings**

FISH BAKE

- 1 cup Original Bisquick® mix
- ½ teaspoon salt, if desired
- 1 teaspoon smoked Spanish paprika
- ½ to 1 teaspoon chipotle chile powder
- ½ teaspoon lemon-pepper seasoning
- ½ cup evaporated milk
- 6 tilapia fillets (1½ lb)
  Cooking spray

SALSA

- 4 slices smoked thick-sliced bacon, crisply cooked, crumbled
- 2 avocados, pitted, peeled and chopped
- 2 cups diced seeded tomatoes (about 2 large)
- ⅓ cup chopped red onion
- ¼ cup chopped fresh cilantro
- 2 tablespoons lime juice
- ½ teaspoon salt
- ¼ teaspoon freshly ground pepper

1 Heat oven to 375°F. Spray 13x9-inch (3-quart) glass baking dish with cooking spray.

2 In shallow dish, mix Bisquick mix, salt, paprika, chile powder and lemon-pepper seasoning. In another shallow dish, place evaporated milk.

3 Dip fish in milk, then coat with Bisquick mixture. Place fish in baking dish. Spray tops of fish with cooking spray to moisten.

4 Bake 15 to 20 minutes or until fish flakes easily with fork.

5 Meanwhile, in large bowl, mix salsa ingredients. Let stand 10 to 15 minutes. Stir well; taste and adjust seasoning as needed.

6 To serve, place fish on 6 warm plates; top each with a spoonful of salsa.

1 Serving: Calories 340; Total Fat 15g (Saturated Fat 3.5g; Trans Fat 1g); Cholesterol 70mg; Sodium 740mg; Total Carbohydrate 22g (Dietary Fiber 5g); Protein 28g **Exchanges:** 1½ Starch, 3 Medium-Fat Meat **Carbohydrate Choices:** 1½

Fish with Tomato-Bacon-Avocado Salsa developed by Peter Halferty, Corpus Christi, TX, won honorable mention in our Better with Bisquick Contest.

Substitute 2 egg whites mixed with 2 teaspoons water for the evaporated milk.

CHAPTER 5

Make Room for Dessert

Impossibly Easy Salted Caramel Apple Mini Pies

Prep Time: 15 Minutes • **Start to Finish:** 35 Minutes • 12 mini pies

FILLING

1½ cups diced peeled (¼-inch) Granny Smith apples

¾ teaspoon ground cinnamon

⅛ teaspoon ground nutmeg

BATTER

½ cup Original Bisquick® mix

⅓ cup sugar

⅓ cup milk

2 tablespoons butter, melted

1 egg

TOPPING

¾ cup sweetened whipped cream

½ cup caramel topping

¼ cup chopped toasted* pecans

Coarse sea salt, if desired

1 Heat oven to 375°F. Place paper baking cup in each of 12 regular-size muffin cups; spray cups with cooking spray.

2 In small bowl, mix filling ingredients; set aside.

3 In another small bowl, stir batter ingredients with whisk or fork until blended. Spoon 1 level measuring tablespoon batter into each muffin cup. Top with 2 measuring tablespoons apple mixture. Spoon 1 level measuring tablespoon batter over apples in each muffin cup.

4 Bake 15 minutes or until set in center and edges are golden brown. Cool 5 minutes. Remove muffins from pan to cooling rack. To serve, remove paper baking cups, if desired. Place each pie in small individual serving bowl; top with 1 tablespoon whipped cream, 2 teaspoons caramel sauce, 1 teaspoon pecans and a sprinkle of salt.

*To toast pecans, cook in an ungreased skillet over medium heat 5 to 7 minutes, stirring frequently, until golden brown.

1 Mini Pie: Calories 140; Total Fat 6g (Saturated Fat 2.5g; Trans Fat 0g); Cholesterol 25mg; Sodium 140mg; Total Carbohydrate 21g (Dietary Fiber 0g); Protein 1g **Exchanges:** ½ Starch, 1 Other Carbohydrate, 1 Fat **Carbohydrate Choices:** 1½

Bourbon Apple Pie

Prep Time: 15 Minutes • **Start to Finish:** 2 Hours 45 Minutes • 8 servings

CRUST

1½ cups Original Bisquick® mix

¼ cup butter, softened

3 tablespoons boiling water

FILLING

1 can (21 oz) apple pie filling

3 tablespoons bourbon

TOPPING

1 cup Original Bisquick® mix

½ cup packed brown sugar

3 tablespoons cold butter

DRIZZLE

⅓ cup powdered sugar

2 teaspoons whipping cream

2 teaspoons bourbon

1 Heat oven to 375°F. In medium bowl, mix 1½ cups Bisquick mix and ¼ cup softened butter with fork until crumbly. Add boiling water; stir vigorously with fork until dough forms. Gather into ball. Press firmly and evenly against bottom and up side of ungreased 9-inch glass pie plate; flute edge.

2 In medium bowl, gently stir filling ingredients until blended. Spoon mixture evenly into crust.

3 In small bowl, mix 1 cup Bisquick mix and the brown sugar. Cut in 3 tablespoons cold butter with pastry blender or fork until mixture looks like coarse crumbs (streusel will look dry). Sprinkle over filling.

4 Bake 15 minutes. Cover top of pie with foil; bake 10 to 15 minutes longer or until golden brown. Cool 2 to 3 hours before serving.

5 In small bowl, stir drizzle ingredients until smooth; drizzle over cooled pie (don't be tempted to drizzle over hot or very warm pie; it will melt into the streusel).

1 Serving: Calories 420; Total Fat 16g (Saturated Fat 8g; Trans Fat 1.5g); Cholesterol 30mg; Sodium 580mg; Total Carbohydrate 63g (Dietary Fiber 1g); Protein 3g
Carbohydrate Choices: 4

Dulce de Leche Banana-Rum Pie

Prep Time: 15 Minutes • **Start to Finish:** 3 Hours 55 Minutes • 10 servings

1 cup mashed ripe bananas (2 medium)

2 teaspoons lemon juice

⅓ cup Original Bisquick® mix

¼ cup sugar

3 tablespoons butter, melted

3 tablespoons dark rum

1 can (14 oz) sweetened condensed milk (not evaporated)

2 eggs

1½ cups frozen (thawed) whipped topping

½ cup dulce de leche milk caramel spread

4 chocolate-filled tubular-shaped pirouette cookies, coarsely crushed

1 Heat oven to 350°F. Spray 9-inch glass pie plate with cooking spray. In small bowl, mix bananas and lemon juice; set aside.

2 In medium bowl, stir Bisquick mix, sugar, butter, 2 tablespoons of the rum, the condensed milk and eggs until blended. Add banana mixture; stir until blended. Pour into pie plate.

3 Bake 35 to 40 minutes or until center is set. Cool completely on cooling rack, about 1 hour. Cover; refrigerate 2 hours or until well chilled.

4 Spread whipped topping over pie to within ½ inch of edge. In small microwavable bowl, microwave caramel spread uncovered on High 30 to 45 seconds or until thoroughly heated; stir in remaining 1 tablespoon rum. Drizzle over pie. Garnish with cookies. Store covered in refrigerator.

1 Serving: Calories 340; Total Fat 12g (Saturated Fat 8g; Trans Fat 0g); Cholesterol 0mg; Sodium 170mg; Total Carbohydrate 51g (Dietary Fiber 0g); Protein 6g **Exchanges:** 2 Fat **Carbohydrate Choices:** 3½

Gluten-Free Impossibly Easy Pumpkin Pie

Prep Time: 10 Minutes • **Start to Finish:** 4 Hours 20 Minutes • 6 servings

1¼ cups canned pumpkin (not pumpkin pie mix)

½ cup Bisquick® Gluten Free mix

½ cup sugar

¾ cup evaporated milk

1 tablespoon butter, softened

1½ teaspoons pumpkin pie spice

1 teaspoon gluten-free vanilla

2 eggs

Whipped topping, if desired

1 Heat oven to 350°F. Spray 9-inch glass pie plate with cooking spray (without flour).

2 In large bowl, stir all ingredients except whipped topping with whisk until blended. Pour into pie plate.

3 Bake 35 to 38 minutes or until knife inserted in center comes out clean. Cool 30 minutes. Refrigerate about 3 hours or until well chilled. Serve with whipped topping. Store covered in refrigerator.

1 Serving: Calories 200; Total Fat 5g (Saturated Fat 2.5g; Trans Fat 0g); Cholesterol 70mg; Sodium 190mg; Total Carbohydrate 33g (Dietary Fiber 2g); Protein 5g **Exchanges:** 1½ Starch, ½ Other Carbohydrate, 1 Fat **Carbohydrate Choices:** 2

> If you are cooking gluten free, always read labels to make sure each recipe ingredient is gluten free. Products and ingredient sources can change.
>
> To lower the fat content a bit, substitute fat-free evaporated milk for evaporated milk.

Gluten-Free Creamy Chocolate Pie

Prep Time: 1 Hour 10 Minutes • **Start to Finish:** 6 Hours 30 Minutes • **10 servings**

CRUST

- 1 cup Bisquick® Gluten Free mix
- 5 tablespoons cold butter
- 3 tablespoons water

FILLING

- ¼ cup granulated sugar
- 3 tablespoons cornstarch
- 1¼ cups milk
- 1 cup semisweet chocolate chips
- 1 teaspoon gluten-free vanilla
- 1¼ cups whipping cream
- 1 tablespoon powdered sugar

If you are cooking gluten free, always read labels to make sure each recipe ingredient is gluten free. Products and ingredient sources can change.

1 Heat oven to 425°F. Grease 9-inch glass pie plate with shortening or cooking spray (without flour). Coarsely chop 1 tablespoon of the chocolate chips for topping; set aside.

2 In medium bowl, place Bisquick mix. Cut in butter with pastry blender or fork until mixture looks like fine crumbs. Stir in water; shape into ball with hands. Press dough in bottom and up side of pie plate.

3 Bake 10 to 12 minutes or until lightly browned. Cool completely, about 30 minutes.

4 Meanwhile, in 2-quart saucepan, mix granulated sugar and cornstarch. Gradually stir in milk; cook over medium heat until mixture boils, stirring constantly. Add remaining chocolate chips and the vanilla, stirring until melted and smooth. Pour into medium bowl; cover surface with plastic wrap. Refrigerate 30 minutes or until chilled.

5 Beat cooled chocolate mixture with electric mixer on medium speed about 2 minutes or until smooth and creamy. In large bowl, beat whipping cream and powdered sugar with electric mixer on high speed until stiff peaks form; reserve 1 cup for topping. Gently stir chocolate mixture into remaining whipped cream mixture. Spoon evenly into cooled baked crust. Pipe reserved whipped cream around edge of pie; sprinkle with reserved chopped chocolate chips. Refrigerate 6 to 8 hours or until set. Cut into wedges to serve. Store covered in refrigerator.

1 Serving: Calories 330; Total Fat 21g (Saturated Fat 13g; Trans Fat 0.5g); Cholesterol 50mg; Sodium 200mg; Total Carbohydrate 31g (Dietary Fiber 1g); Protein 3g **Exchanges:** 1 Starch, 1 Other Carbohydrate, 4 Fat **Carbohydrate Choices:** 2

Miniature semisweet chocolate chips can be used, instead of chopping the chocolate chips, to garnish each piece of pie.

Impossibly Easy Butterscotch-Pecan Pie

Prep Time: 10 Minutes • **Start to Finish:** 1 Hour • 8 servings

1 cup milk

¼ cup butter, softened

1 teaspoon vanilla

2 eggs

1 cup packed brown sugar

½ cup Original Bisquick® mix

1 cup chopped pecans

Sweetened whipped cream, if desired

1 Heat oven to 350°F. Spray 9-inch glass pie plate with cooking spray.

2 In blender, place all ingredients except pecans and whipped cream. Cover; blend on high speed about 1 minute or until smooth. (Or beat in medium bowl with electric mixer on high speed 2 minutes.) Pour into pie plate. Sprinkle with pecans.

3 Bake 28 to 30 minutes or until set and knife inserted in center comes out clean. Cool on cooling rack at least 20 minutes. Serve warm or cold with whipped cream. Store covered in refrigerator.

1 Serving: Calories 420; Total Fat 28g (Saturated Fat 10g; Trans Fat 1g); Cholesterol 105mg; Sodium 200mg; Total Carbohydrate 38g (Dietary Fiber 1g); Protein 5g **Exchanges:** 1½ Starch, 1 Other Carbohydrate, 5½ Fat **Carbohydrate Choices:** 2½

Gluten-Free Impossibly Easy Coconut Pie

Prep Time: 10 Minutes • **Start to Finish:** 3 Hours • 8 servings

3 eggs
1¾ cups milk
¼ cup butter, melted
1½ teaspoons gluten-free vanilla
1 cup flaked or shredded coconut
¾ cup sugar
½ cup Bisquick® Gluten Free mix

1 Heat oven to 350°F. Grease 9-inch glass pie plate with shortening or cooking spray (without flour).

2 In large bowl, stir all ingredients until blended. Pour into pie plate.

3 Bake 45 to 50 minutes or until golden brown and knife inserted in center comes out clean. Cool 2 hours on cooling rack. Cut into wedges. Store covered in refrigerator.

1 Serving: Calories 260; Total Fat 13g (Saturated Fat 8g; Trans Fat 0g); Cholesterol 100mg; Sodium 180mg; Total Carbohydrate 32g (Dietary Fiber 0g); Protein 4g
Exchanges: ½ Starch, 1½ Other Carbohydrate, 2½ Fat **Carbohydrate Choices:** 2

If you are cooking gluten free, always read labels to make sure each recipe ingredient is gluten free. Products and ingredient sources can change.

Two of the most common types of coconut available are flaked and shredded. Flaked coconut is cut into small pieces and is drier than shredded coconut. Either type works well in most recipes, but using shredded results in a more moist and chewy finished product.

French Peach Tart

Prep Time: 30 Minutes • **Start to Finish:** 1 Hour 15 Minutes • **10 servings**

2 tablespoons Original Bisquick® mix

2 cups Original Bisquick® mix

⅓ cup granulated sugar

⅓ cup butter, softened

1 egg

¾ cup whipping cream

⅓ cup sour cream

¼ cup powdered sugar

1 teaspoon vanilla

5 to 6 cups sliced peeled fresh or frozen (thawed) peaches

⅓ cup apple jelly, melted

1 Heat oven to 375°F. Spray cookie sheet with cooking spray; lightly sprinkle with 2 tablespoons Bisquick mix.

2 In medium bowl, mix 2 cups Bisquick mix and the granulated sugar. Cut in butter with pastry blender or fork until mixture looks like coarse crumbs. Stir in egg until soft dough forms. On cookie sheet, roll dough into 12x10-inch rectangle; pinch edges to form ½-inch rim.

3 Bake 8 to 10 minutes or until edges are golden brown. Cool 2 minutes. With large spatula, remove crust to cooling rack; cool completely, about 30 minutes.

4 In chilled medium deep bowl, beat whipping cream, sour cream, powdered sugar and vanilla with electric mixer on medium speed 2 to 3 minutes or until stiff peaks form. Spread whipped cream mixture evenly over crust. Arrange peach slices over whipped cream mixture. Brush with jelly. Serve immediately or refrigerate until serving. Store in refrigerator.

1 Serving: Calories 330; Total Fat 17g (Saturated Fat 9g; Trans Fat 0g); Cholesterol 0mg; Sodium 370mg; Total Carbohydrate 42g (Dietary Fiber 1g); Protein 4g **Exchanges:** 1 Starch, ½ Fruit, 1½ Other Carbohydrate, 3 Fat **Carbohydrate Choices:** 3

Peach Cobbler

Prep Time: 10 Minutes • **Start to Finish:** 1 Hour 20 Minutes • **6 servings**

1 cup Original Bisquick® mix

½ teaspoon ground nutmeg

1 cup milk

½ cup butter, melted

1 cup sugar

1 can (29 oz) sliced peaches, drained

1 Heat oven to 375°F. In ungreased 8-inch square (2-quart) glass baking dish, stir Bisquick mix, nutmeg and milk with whisk or fork until blended. Stir in butter until blended.

2 In medium bowl, stir sugar and peaches until peaches are coated with sugar. Spoon over batter in baking dish.

3 Bake 50 to 60 minutes or until golden brown. Let stand 10 minutes before serving. Serve warm.

1 Serving: Calories 410; Total Fat 19g (Saturated Fat 11g; Trans Fat 1g); Cholesterol 45mg; Sodium 400mg; Total Carbohydrate 55g (Dietary Fiber 2g); Protein 3g **Exchanges:** 1 Starch, ½ Fruit, 2 Other Carbohydrate, 4 Fat **Carbohydrate Choices:** 3½

Add sparkle to the top of the pie by sprinkling coarse decorating sugar over the dough before baking.

Serve warm cobbler with ice cream, a drizzle of caramel topping and a sprinkling of toasted pecans.

Gluten-Free Cherry-Chip Cobbler

Prep Time: 15 Minutes • **Start to Finish:** 55 Minutes • **6 servings**

FRUIT MIXTURE

- 1 can (21 oz) gluten-free cherry pie filling
- 2 tablespoons orange juice
- ½ teaspoon almond extract

TOPPING

- 1 cup Bisquick® Gluten Free mix
- 1 cup whipping cream
- 2 tablespoons sugar
- 2 tablespoons butter, softened
- ¼ cup miniature semisweet chocolate chips
- ½ teaspoon sugar

1 Heat oven to 350°F. In ungreased 1½-quart microwavable casserole, mix pie filling, orange juice and almond extract. Microwave uncovered on High about 4 minutes or until bubbly around edge; stir.

2 In medium bowl, mix all topping ingredients except ½ teaspoon sugar with spoon until stiff dough forms. Drop dough by 6 spoonfuls (about ¼ cup each) onto warm fruit mixture. Sprinkle ½ teaspoon sugar over dough.

3 Bake 35 to 40 minutes or until topping is golden brown. Serve warm.

1 Serving: Calories 480; Total Fat 19g (Saturated Fat 11g; Trans Fat 0.5g); Cholesterol 55mg; Sodium 270mg; Total Carbohydrate 75g (Dietary Fiber 3g); Protein 3g **Exchanges:** 2 Starch, 3 Other Carbohydrate, 3½ Fat **Carbohydrate Choices:** 5

> If you are cooking gluten free, always read labels to make sure each recipe ingredient is gluten free. Products and ingredient sources can change.
>
> For double the chocolate flavor, stir in ¼ cup chopped white chocolate with the miniature semisweet chocolate chips.

Blackberry Dumpling Cobbler

Prep Time: 20 Minutes • **Start to Finish:** 55 Minutes • **12 servings**

2 bags (16 oz each) frozen blackberries

2 cups sugar

¼ cup butter

3 packages (8 oz each) ⅓-less-fat cream cheese (Neufchâtel), softened

⅔ cup fat-free (skim) milk

2¼ cups Original Bisquick® mix

¾ cup old-fashioned oats

Vanilla ice cream, if desired

1 Heat oven to 350°F. Lightly grease 13x9-inch (3-quart) glass baking dish with shortening or cooking spray.

2 In 3-quart saucepan, heat blackberries, 1⅓ cups of the sugar and the butter to boiling over medium heat, stirring gently until butter is melted and sugar is dissolved. Remove from heat; set aside.

3 In large bowl, beat cream cheese and remaining ⅔ cup sugar with electric mixer on medium speed until fluffy. Beat in milk until smooth. Stir in Bisquick mix and oats. Spread two-thirds of the cream cheese mixture (about 3 cups) in baking dish; spoon blackberry mixture evenly over top. Spoon remaining cream cheese mixture over blackberry mixture.

4 Bake 33 to 37 minutes or until filling is bubbly and topping is golden brown. Serve warm with ice cream.

1 Serving: Calories 429; Total Fat 16g (Saturated Fat 9g; Trans Fat 0g); Cholesterol 0mg; Sodium 586mg; Total Carbohydrate 68g (Dietary Fiber 4g); Protein 9g **Exchanges:** 1 Starch, 1 Fruit, 2½ Other Carbohydrate, 1 Medium-Fat Meat, ½ Fat
Carbohydrate Choices: 4½

Sweet Potato Bread Pudding with Orange Sauce

Prep Time: 40 Minutes • **Start to Finish:** 4 Hours • 18 servings

PUDDING

4½	cups Original Bisquick® mix
1⅓	cups milk
1	cup chopped pecans
½	cup raisins
2½	cups milk
2½	cups half-and-half
1¼	cups mashed baked sweet potatoes
1	cup granulated sugar
¼	cup butter, melted
1	tablespoon vanilla
½	teaspoon ground cinnamon
½	teaspoon ground nutmeg
4	eggs

SAUCE

2	cups powdered sugar
1	cup butter, softened
½	cup orange juice
2	teaspoons cornstarch
4	egg yolks, beaten

1 Heat oven to 450°F. In large bowl, stir Bisquick mix and 1⅓ cups milk until soft dough forms. Drop dough by spoonfuls onto ungreased cookie sheet.

2 Bake 8 to 10 minutes or until golden brown. Break up biscuits.

3 Grease bottom and sides of 13x9-inch pan with butter. Arrange biscuit pieces evenly in bottom of pan. Sprinkle with pecans and raisins.

4 In large bowl, beat all remaining pudding ingredients with electric mixer on low speed until blended. Pour over biscuits in pan. Cover; refrigerate at least 2 hours but no longer than 8 hours.

5 Heat oven to 350°F. Gently stir mixture in pan.

6 Bake 55 to 65 minutes or until top is golden brown and toothpick inserted in center comes out clean.

7 Meanwhile, in 2-quart saucepan, heat all sauce ingredients over low heat 5 to 10 minutes, stirring constantly with whisk, until slightly thickened and temperature reaches 165°F for 15 seconds. Serve warm sauce over pudding. Store covered in refrigerator.

1 Serving: Calories 515; Total Fat 29g (Saturated Fat 13g; Trans Fat 0g); Cholesterol 145mg; Sodium 570mg; Total Carbohydrate 56g (Dietary Fiber 2g); Protein 8g
Exchanges: 3 Starch, 1 Other Carbohydrate, 5 Fat **Carbohydrate Choices:** 4

Mini Shortcakes with Strawberries and Rhubarb

Prep Time: 20 Minutes • **Start to Finish:** 40 Minutes • 12 shortcakes

FILLING

- 3 cups cut-up fresh or frozen rhubarb
- 1 cup sugar
- 2 tablespoons cornstarch
- 2 tablespoons cold water
- 2 cups sliced strawberries

SHORTCAKES

- 2⅓ cups Bisquick Heart Smart® mix
- 2 containers (6 oz each) vanilla fat-free yogurt
- 2 to 3 tablespoons sugar
- 2 to 3 tablespoons butter, melted

1 In 2-quart saucepan, heat rhubarb and 1 cup sugar to boiling; reduce heat. Mix cornstarch and 2 tablespoons cold water; stir into rhubarb mixture. Simmer uncovered 5 to 7 minutes, stirring occasionally, until rhubarb is tender and mixture is slightly thickened. Cool sauce about 30 minutes. Stir in strawberries. Cover; refrigerate until ready to serve.

2 Heat oven to 425°F. In medium bowl, mix Bisquick mix, 1 container of the yogurt, 2 to 3 tablespoons sugar and the melted butter until soft dough forms. Drop dough by heaping tablespoonfuls onto ungreased cookie sheet to make 12 shortcakes.

3 Bake 8 to 10 minutes or until golden brown. Split warm shortcakes; top with about 3 tablespoons rhubarb mixture and about 1 tablespoon remaining yogurt.

1 Shortcake: Calories 220; Total Fat 3.5g (Saturated Fat 1.5g; Trans Fat 0g); Cholesterol 5mg; Sodium 230mg; Total Carbohydrate 43g (Dietary Fiber 1g); Protein 3g **Exchanges:** 1 Starch, 1½ Other Carbohydrate, ½ Vegetable, ½ Fat **Carbohydrate Choices:** 3

Lemon-Berry Shortcakes

Prep Time: 20 Minutes • **Start to Finish:** 35 Minutes • 5 shortcakes

¼ cup sugar

2 tablespoons grated lemon peel

¼ cup blueberry preserves or jam

1 tablespoon water

2 tablespoons fresh lemon juice

1½ cups fresh strawberries, quartered

1½ cups fresh blueberries

1¾ cups Bisquick Heart Smart® mix

⅓ cup plus 1 tablespoon 1% (low-fat) milk

5 tablespoons frozen (thawed) fat-free whipped topping

1 Heat oven to 425°F. Spray cookie sheet with cooking spray. In small bowl, mix sugar and lemon peel.

2 In 12-inch skillet, heat preserves and water over medium heat until preserves are melted. Stir in 1 tablespoon of the sugar mixture, the lemon juice, strawberries and blueberries. Cook 1 minute, stirring constantly, until sugar is dissolved. Remove from heat; set aside.

3 In medium bowl, stir Bisquick mix, milk and remaining sugar mixture just until moistened.

4 Place dough on surface lightly sprinkled with Bisquick mix; pat dough to ½-inch thickness. With 2½-inch round cutter, cut dough into 5 rounds. Place 1 inch apart on cookie sheet.

5 Bake 10 to 12 minutes or until golden brown. Split shortcakes; spoon berry mixture evenly over bottom half of each shortcake. Top each with 1 tablespoon whipped topping; cover with shortcake tops.

1 Shortcake: Calories 269; Total Fat 3g (Saturated Fat 0g; Trans Fat 0g); Cholesterol 0mg; Sodium 430mg; Total Carbohydrate 59g (Dietary Fiber 3g); Protein 4g **Exchanges:** 1 Starch, 1 Fruit, 2 Other Carbohydrate, ½ Fat **Carbohydrate Choices:** 4

Ginger-Pear Shortcakes

Prep Time: 25 Minutes • **Start to Finish:** 50 Minutes • 12 shortcakes

SHORTCAKES

2½ cups Original Bisquick® mix

1 tablespoon granulated sugar

½ cup plus 2 tablespoons milk

2 tablespoons molasses

¼ cup chopped walnuts

3 tablespoons chopped crystallized ginger

1 tablespoon butter, melted

¼ teaspoon ground cinnamon

¼ teaspoon ground cloves

FILLING

6 Bosc pears, peeled, sliced

2 tablespoons lemon juice

3 tablespoons butter

3 tablespoons packed brown sugar

3 teaspoons vanilla

⅛ teaspoon salt

Sweetened whipped cream, if desired

1 Heat oven to 375°F. Spray cookie sheet with cooking spray.

2 In large bowl, stir Bisquick mix, granulated sugar, milk and molasses until soft dough forms.

3 Place dough on surface sprinkled with Bisquick mix; gently roll in Bisquick mix to coat. Knead 3 to 4 times. Pat dough to ¼-inch thickness. With 2¾-inch round cutter, cut dough into 12 rounds. Place 1 inch apart on cookie sheet.

4 In small bowl, mix walnuts, ginger, melted butter, cinnamon and cloves. Divide mixture evenly over biscuit tops; lightly press into dough.

5 Bake 12 minutes or until lightly browned. Remove from cookie sheet to cooling rack; cool completely.

6 In large bowl, toss pears and lemon juice. In 12-inch skillet, melt 3 tablespoons butter over medium-high heat. Add pear mixture; stir to coat with butter. Cook 2 minutes; sprinkle with brown sugar. Heat to boiling; reduce heat to low. Simmer uncovered 5 minutes, stirring occasionally, until pears are soft and sauce thickens slightly. Remove from heat. Stir in vanilla and salt.

7 To serve, split shortcakes. Place shortcake bottoms on dessert plates; top with pear mixture, whipped cream and shortcake tops.

1 Shortcake: Calories 250; Total Fat 10g (Saturated Fat 3.5g; Trans Fat 0g); Cholesterol 0mg; Sodium 380mg; Total Carbohydrate 40g (Dietary Fiber 2g); Protein 3g **Exchanges:** 1 Starch, ½ Fruit, 1 Other Carbohydrate, 2 Fat **Carbohydrate Choices:** 2½

Fudgy Caramel Shortcake Shooters

Prep Time: 30 Minutes • **Start to Finish:** 45 Minutes • 12 shooters

1 cup plus 2 tablespoons Original Bisquick® mix

2 tablespoons sugar

2 tablespoons unsweetened baking cocoa

⅓ cup milk

2 tablespoons butter, melted

⅓ cup miniature semisweet chocolate chips

3 cups frozen (thawed) whipped topping

6 tablespoons butterscotch caramel topping

Additional miniature semisweet chocolate chips, if desired

Coarse sea salt, if desired

1 Heat oven to 400°F. Spray 24 mini muffin cups with cooking spray.

2 In medium bowl, stir Bisquick mix, sugar and cocoa with whisk until blended and no lumps remain. Add milk and melted butter; stir just until moistened. Stir in ⅓ cup chocolate chips. Divide batter evenly among muffin cups.

3 Bake 5 to 7 minutes or until tops spring back when lightly touched and toothpick inserted in center comes out almost clean. Cool 5 minutes. Gently loosen sides of shortcakes from pan; remove to cooling rack. Cool completely.

4 For each shooter, spoon 2 tablespoons whipped topping into 3x2-inch shot glass. Top with 1 teaspoon caramel topping, 1 shortcake, 2 tablespoons whipped topping and 1 more shortcake. Drizzle with ½ teaspoon caramel topping. Garnish with chocolate chips; sprinkle lightly with salt.

1 Shooter: Calories 190; Total Fat 9g (Saturated Fat 6g; Trans Fat 0.5g); Cholesterol 5mg; Sodium 200mg; Total Carbohydrate 24g (Dietary Fiber 1g); Protein 2g **Exchanges:** ½ Starch, 1 Other Carbohydrate, 2 Fat **Carbohydrate Choices:** 1½

> Substitute 12 paper cups (5-oz size) for the shot glasses.
>
> To make Fudgy Salted Rum-Caramel Shortcakes, stir 1 teaspoon rum into the caramel sauce before assembling the shooters.

S'more Shortcake Pops

Prep Time: 25 Minutes • Start to Finish: 1 Hour 25 Minutes • 36 shortcake pops

2⅓ cups Original Bisquick® mix

⅔ cup milk

3 tablespoons sugar

3 tablespoons butter or margarine, melted

36 craft sticks (flat wooden sticks with rounded ends)

2 cups milk chocolate chips (12 oz)

1 teaspoon shortening

2 tablespoons graham cracker crumbs

1 block polystyrene foam

1 Heat oven to 425°F. In medium bowl, stir Bisquick mix, milk, sugar and butter until soft dough forms. Drop by 6 spoonfuls onto ungreased cookie sheet.

2 Bake 10 to 12 minutes or until golden brown. Remove from cookie sheet to cooling rack. Cool completely, about 30 minutes.

3 Crumble shortcake into large bowl. Add marshmallow creme; mix with spoon until dough forms. Shape into 36 (1-inch) balls (mixture will be sticky). Place on cookie sheet. Insert 1 craft stick halfway into each shortcake ball; gently squeeze dough around stick. Freeze 15 minutes.

4 Meanwhile, in medium microwavable bowl, microwave chocolate chips and shortening uncovered on High 1 minute, stirring once, until melted and smooth.

5 Remove shortcake balls from freezer a few at a time. Gently dip each ball two-thirds of the way into chocolate mixture; tap off excess. Sprinkle with graham cracker crumbs. Poke opposite end of stick into foam block. Let stand until set. Store pops covered in refrigerator. To serve, uncover pops; let stand at room temperature 15 minutes.

1 Shortcake Pop: Calories 110; Total Fat 5g (Saturated Fat 2.5g, Trans Fat 0g); Cholesterol 5mg; Sodium 115mg; Total Carbohydrate 15g (Dietary Fiber 0g); Protein 1g **Exchanges:** ½ Starch, ½ Other Carbohydrate, 1 Fat **Carbohydrate Choices:** 1

Raspberry Streusel Snack Cake

Prep Time: 15 Minutes • **Start to Finish:** 1 Hour 55 Minutes • **9 servings**

2½ cups Original Bisquick® mix

¾ cup milk

½ cup granulated sugar

2 tablespoons butter, melted

1 teaspoon vanilla

1 egg

1 cup frozen raspberries (do not thaw)

1 tablespoon all-purpose flour

½ cup packed brown sugar

3 tablespoons cold butter

½ cup coarsely chopped pecans

Powdered sugar, if desired

1 Heat oven to 350°F. Spray 9-inch square pan with cooking spray.

2 In large bowl, beat 2 cups of the Bisquick mix, the milk, granulated sugar, 2 tablespoons butter, the vanilla and egg with electric mixer on low speed 30 seconds. Beat on medium speed 2 minutes. Pour into pan. In small bowl, toss frozen raspberries with flour. Sprinkle over batter.

3 In small bowl, mix remaining ½ cup Bisquick mix and the brown sugar. Cut in 3 tablespoons butter, with pastry blender or fork, until mixture looks like coarse crumbs. Stir in pecans. Sprinkle over batter.

4 Bake 35 to 40 minutes or until toothpick inserted in center comes out clean. Cool completely in pan on cooling rack, about 1 hour. Cut into 3 rows by 3 rows. Sprinkle with powdered sugar.

1 Serving: Calories 350; Total Fat 16g (Saturated Fat 6g; Trans Fat 0g); Cholesterol 0mg; Sodium 480mg; Total Carbohydrate 49g (Dietary Fiber 2g); Protein 5g **Exchanges:** 1½ Starch, 1½ Other Carbohydrate, 2½ Fat **Carbohydrate Choices:** 3

Cream Cheese Pound Cake

Prep Time: 15 Minutes • **Start to Finish:** 3 Hours 35 Minutes • 16 servings

3 cups Original Bisquick® mix

1½ cups granulated sugar

½ cup all-purpose flour

¾ cup butter, softened

1 teaspoon vanilla

⅛ teaspoon salt

6 eggs

1 package (8 oz) cream cheese, softened

Powdered sugar, if desired

1 Heat oven to 350°F. Grease 12-cup fluted tube cake pan, 10-inch angel food (tube) cake pan or 2 (9x5-inch) loaf pans with shortening; lightly flour.

2 In large bowl, beat all ingredients except powdered sugar with electric mixer on low speed 30 seconds, scraping bowl frequently. Beat on medium speed 4 minutes, scraping bowl occasionally. Pour into pan.

3 Bake 55 to 60 minutes or until toothpick inserted near center comes out clean. Cool 20 minutes; remove from pan to cooling rack. Cool completely, about 2 hours. Sprinkle with powdered sugar.

1 Serving: Calories 335; Total Fat 19g (Saturated Fat 10g; Trans Fat 0g); Cholesterol 120mg; Sodium 460mg; Total Carbohydrate 36g (Dietary Fiber 0g); Protein 5g **Exchanges:** ½ Starch, 2 Other Carbohydrate, ½ Medium-Fat Meat, 3 Fat **Carbohydrate Choices:** 2½

> For a hint of lemon, use lemon extract instead of the vanilla.

Glazed Lemon Pound Cake

Prep Time: 15 Minutes • **Start to Finish:** 2 Hours 15 Minutes • **12 servings**

CAKE

2½ cups Original Bisquick® mix

⅔ cup granulated sugar

¼ cup butter, melted

3 eggs

¾ cup milk

1 teaspoon vanilla

3 tablespoons grated lemon peel

GLAZE

½ cup powdered sugar

1 tablespoon lemon juice

1 Heat oven to 325°F. Spray bottom only of 9x5-inch loaf pan with baking spray with flour.

2 In large bowl, beat all cake ingredients except lemon peel with electric mixer on low speed 30 seconds, scraping bowl constantly. Beat on medium speed 2 minutes, scraping bowl occasionally. Stir in lemon peel. Pour into pan.

3 Bake 45 to 50 minutes or until toothpick inserted in center comes out clean. Cool 10 minutes. Run knife or metal spatula around sides of pan to loosen cake; remove from pan to cooling rack. Cool completely, about 1 hour.

4 In small bowl, mix powdered sugar and lemon juice with spoon until smooth. Drizzle glaze over cake.

1 Serving: Calories 230; Total Fat 9g (Saturated Fat 4g; Trans Fat 1g); Cholesterol 65mg; Sodium 360mg; Total Carbohydrate 34g (Dietary Fiber 0g); Protein 4g **Exchanges:** 1 Starch, 1½ Other Carbohydrate, 1½ Fat **Carbohydrate Choices:** 2

> To make Glazed Lime Pound Cake, substitute 3 tablespoons grated lime peel and 1 tablespoon lime juice for the lemon peel and lemon juice.

Easy Pumpkin Cheesecake

Prep Time: 10 Minutes • **Start to Finish:** 4 Hours 55 Minutes • 8 servings

1 can (15 oz) pumpkin (not pumpkin pie mix)

1 package (8 oz) cream cheese, cut into 16 pieces, softened

¼ teaspoon vanilla

3 eggs

¾ cup sugar

½ cup Original Bisquick® mix

1½ teaspoons pumpkin pie spice

1 cup caramel topping, if desired

Pecan halves, if desired

1 Heat oven to 350°F. Spray 9-inch glass pie plate with cooking spray.

2 In blender, place all ingredients except caramel topping and pecan halves. Cover; blend on high speed about 2 minutes or until smooth. (Or beat in medium bowl with electric mixer on high speed 2 minutes.) Pour into pie plate.

3 Bake 43 to 47 minutes or just until puffed and center is dry (do not overbake). Cool completely on cooling rack, about 1 hour. Refrigerate at least 3 hours until chilled. Cut into wedges. Drizzle individual servings with caramel topping; garnish with pecan halves. Store covered in refrigerator up to 3 days.

1 Serving: Calories 250; Total Fat 13g (Saturated Fat 6g; Trans Fat 0g); Cholesterol 0mg; Sodium 210mg; Total Carbohydrate 30g (Dietary Fiber 2g); Protein 5g **Exchanges:** ½ Starch, ½ Fruit, 1 Other Carbohydrate, 2½ Fat **Carbohydrate Choices:** 2

Substitute ¾ teaspoon each ground cinnamon and nutmeg for the pumpkin pie spice.

Velvet Crumb Cake

Prep Time: 20 Minutes • **Start to Finish:** 1 Hour • 8 servings

CAKE

1½ cups Original Bisquick® mix

½ cup granulated sugar

½ cup milk or water

2 tablespoons shortening

1 teaspoon vanilla

1 egg

TOPPING

½ cup flaked coconut

⅓ cup packed brown sugar

¼ cup chopped nuts

3 tablespoons butter, softened

2 tablespoons milk

1 Heat oven to 350°F. Grease 9-inch round or 8-inch square pan with shortening; lightly flour.

2 In large bowl, beat Bisquick mix, granulated sugar, ½ cup milk, the shortening, vanilla and egg with electric mixer on low speed 30 seconds, scraping bowl constantly. Beat on medium speed 4 minutes, scraping bowl occasionally. Pour into pan.

3 Bake 30 to 35 minutes or until toothpick inserted in center comes out clean. Cool 5 minutes.

4 In small bowl, mix coconut, brown sugar, nuts, butter and 2 tablespoons milk. Spread topping over cake.

5 Set oven to broil. Broil cake with top about 3 inches from heat 2 to 3 minutes or until golden brown. Serve warm or cool completely.

1 Serving: Calories 320; Total Fat 16g (Saturated Fat 6g; Trans Fat 1.5g); Cholesterol 40mg; Sodium 340mg; Total Carbohydrate 40g (Dietary Fiber 0g); Protein 4g
Exchanges: 1 Starch, 1½ Other Carbohydrate, 3 Fat **Carbohydrate Choices:** 2½

If you're chopping nuts in a food processor, use quick pulses for the best results. Go ahead and chop more nuts than you need. Wrap and freeze the extra nuts to use later.

Add a handful of chocolate chips or butterscotch chips to the topping for a decadent finish.

Mini Rainbow Whoopie Pies

Prep Time: 2 Hours • **Start to Finish:** 2 Hours • **50 mini whoopie pies**

COOKIES

- 2 tablespoons butter, softened
- ½ cup granulated sugar
- 1½ cups Original Bisquick® mix
- 1 egg
- ⅓ cup milk
- 1 teaspoon vanilla
  Red, yellow, green and blue food colors

FILLING

- 4 oz (half of 8-oz package) cream cheese, softened
- ¼ cup butter, softened
- ½ teaspoon vanilla
- 1¼ cups powdered sugar

1 Heat oven to 350°F. Line large cookie sheets with cooking parchment paper.

2 In medium bowl, beat 2 tablespoons butter and the granulated sugar with electric mixer on low speed until well blended and sandy in texture. Add Bisquick mix, egg, milk and 1 teaspoon vanilla. Beat on medium speed 2 minutes, scraping bowl occasionally, until smooth. Divide batter evenly among 5 small bowls (about ⅓ cup each).

3 Stir food color into each as desired to create rainbow colors. Stir until well blended. Spoon batter into individual resealable food-storage plastic bags. Cut ¼ inch off corner of each bag. Onto cookie sheets, squeeze each bag of colored batter gently to make 20 (½-inch) circles of dough (about ¼ teaspoon each), about 1 inch apart.

4 Bake 3 to 5 minutes or until tops spring back when lightly touched. Cool 2 minutes. Gently remove from cookie sheets to cooling racks; cool completely, about 20 minutes.

5 In medium bowl, beat cream cheese, ¼ cup butter and ½ teaspoon vanilla with electric mixer on low speed until well blended. Gradually add powdered sugar, beating on low speed until blended. Increase speed to medium; beat about 1 minute or until smooth.

6 For each whoopie pie, spread about ½ teaspoon filling on bottom of 1 cookie; place second cookie, bottom side down, on filling. Store loosely covered in refrigerator.

1 Mini Whoopie Pie: Calories 60; Total Fat 2.5g (Saturated Fat 1.5g; Trans Fat 0g); Cholesterol 10mg; Sodium 70mg; Total Carbohydrate 8g (Dietary Fiber 0g); Protein 0g **Exchanges:** ½ Other Carbohydrate, ½ Fat **Carbohydrate Choices:** ½

Save time in the kitchen by making larger bite-size whoopie pies. Use about ½ teaspoon dough per cookie. Bake 6 to 7 minutes.

Gel or paste food color makes brighter colors than liquid food color.

Gluten-Free Peanut Blossoms

Prep Time: 30 Minutes • **Start to Finish:** 1 Hour 50 Minutes • **4 dozen cookies**

¾ cup granulated sugar

½ cup packed brown sugar

½ cup peanut butter

¼ cup shortening

¼ cup butter, softened

1 egg

1½ cups Bisquick® Gluten Free mix

48 Hershey's® Kisses® brand milk chocolates, unwrapped

1 In large bowl, mix ½ cup of the granulated sugar, the brown sugar, peanut butter, shortening, butter and egg. Stir in Bisquick mix until dough forms. Cover; refrigerate 1 hour or until firm.

2 Heat oven to 375°F. In small bowl, place remaining ¼ cup granulated sugar. Shape dough into 48 (1-inch) balls; roll in sugar. On ungreased cookie sheets, place balls 2 inches apart.

3 Bake 8 to 10 minutes or until light golden brown. Immediately top each cookie with 1 milk chocolate candy, pressing down firmly so cookie cracks around edge. Remove from cookie sheets to cooling racks.

1 Cookie: Calories 100; Total Fat 5g (Saturated Fat 2g; Trans Fat 0g); Cholesterol 10mg; Sodium 65mg; Total Carbohydrate 12g (Dietary Fiber 0g); Protein 1g **Exchanges:** ½ Starch, ½ Other Carbohydrate, 1 Fat **Carbohydrate Choices:** 1

The HERSHEY'S® KISSES® trademark and trade dress and conical figure and plume device are used under license.

If you are cooking gluten free, always read labels to make sure each recipe ingredient is gluten free. Products and ingredient sources can change.

PB and Chocolate Macadamia Cookies

Prep Time: 35 Minutes • **Start to Finish:** 35 Minutes • **2 dozen cookies**

¾ cup creamy
   peanut butter

2 eggs

2 teaspoons vanilla

1 cup packed brown sugar

2 cups Original
   Bisquick® mix

1 cup semisweet chocolate
   chips (6 oz)

½ cup chopped macadamia
   nuts

1 Heat oven to 350°F. In large bowl, mix peanut butter, eggs and vanilla. Stir in brown sugar until blended. Add Bisquick mix, chocolate chips and nuts, stirring just until moistened. Dough will be crumbly.

2 Shape dough into 24 (1-inch) balls. On ungreased cookie sheets, place balls about 2 inches apart; flatten slightly with fingers or bottom of drinking glass.

3 Bake 10 to 12 minutes or until golden brown. Remove from cookie sheets to cooling racks.

1 Cookie: Calories 205; Total Fat 10g (Saturated Fat 4g; Trans Fat 0g); Cholesterol 0mg; Sodium 181mg; Total Carbohydrate 26g (Dietary Fiber 1g); Protein 4g **Exchanges:** ½ Starch, 1½ Other Carbohydrate, ½ High-Fat Meat, 1 Fat **Carbohydrate Choices:** 2

Gluten-Free Peanut Butter Cookies

Prep Time: 40 Minutes • **Start to Finish:** 2 Hours 40 Minutes • 2½ dozen cookies

½ cup granulated sugar

½ cup packed brown sugar

½ cup peanut butter

¼ cup shortening

¼ cup butter, softened

1 egg

1¼ cups Bisquick® Gluten Free mix

1 In large bowl, mix sugars, peanut butter, shortening, butter and egg. Stir in Bisquick mix. Cover; refrigerate about 2 hours or until firm.

2 Heat oven to 375°F. Shape dough into 30 (1¼-inch) balls. On ungreased cookie sheets, place balls about 3 inches apart. With fork dipped in sugar, flatten balls in crisscross pattern.

3 Bake 9 to 10 minutes or until light golden brown. Cool 5 minutes; remove from cookie sheets to cooling racks.

1 Cookie: Calories 100; Total Fat 6g (Saturated Fat 2g; Trans Fat 0g); Cholesterol 10mg; Sodium 80mg; Total Carbohydrate 11g (Dietary Fiber 0g); Protein 1g **Exchanges:** ½ Other Carbohydrate, 1 Fat **Carbohydrate Choices:** 1

If you are cooking gluten free, always read labels to make sure each recipe ingredient is gluten free. Products and ingredient sources can change.

For a special treat, sandwich two of these all-time favorites together with a scoop of chocolate ice cream. Roll the edge in chopped gluten-free candy bar or nuts.

No-Roll Sugar Cookies

Prep Time: 55 Minutes • **Start to Finish:** 55 Minutes • **4 dozen cookies**

4 cups Original Bisquick® mix

1½ cups powdered sugar

¾ cup butter, softened

1 teaspoon almond extract

2 eggs

1 cup colored or regular granulated sugar

1 Heat oven to 400°F. In large bowl, stir all ingredients except granulated sugar until soft dough forms.

2 Shape dough into 48 (1-inch) balls; roll in colored granulated sugar to coat. On ungreased cookie sheets, place balls about 2 inches apart. Flatten balls slightly with bottom of drinking glass.

3 Bake 5 to 6 minutes or until edges are light golden brown. Cool 1 minute; remove from cookie sheets to cooling racks. Store in tightly covered container.

1 Cookie: Calories 100; Total Fat 4.5g (Saturated Fat 2.5g; Trans Fat 0g); Cholesterol 15mg; Sodium 150mg; Total Carbohydrate 14g (Dietary Fiber 0g); Protein 1g **Exchanges:** ½ Starch, ½ Other Carbohydrate, 1 Fat **Carbohydrate Choices:** 1

> To save time, make cookies as directed—except drop dough by tablespoonfuls about 2 inches apart onto ungreased cookie sheet. Flatten with a sugared drinking glass bottom. (Cookies will be less rounded.)

Simple Ways to Dress Up Sugar Cookies

No-Roll Sugar Cookies (page 305) uses just 6 ingredients to make fresh, homemade cookies. Choose colored sugars to highlight any celebration or add a colorful punch anytime. You can also use regular granulated sugar for everyday cookies—perfect for the cookie jar or tucked inside a bag lunch.

If that's not the way your cookie crumbles, and you're looking for more "wow" factor, try one of these simple ways to decorate the baked cookies (use regular granulated sugar to make the cookies unless noted otherwise).

Sweet Sandwiches—Frost two cookies on the bottom sides with prepared frosting (vanilla or chocolate) and press together. Roll the edge in sprinkles or finely crushed hard candies.

Dab of Decadence—Spoon about 1 teaspoon chocolate frosting onto the center of each cookie and press a thin rectangular chocolate mint half (cut diagonally in half) or other candies into the frosting.

Double Delight—Use colored granulated sugar to make the cookies. Once cooled, add decoration of larger sprinkles for additional color and texture. Attach to cookies with a bit of frosting on the end of a toothpick. Use tweezers to attach the sprinkles to the cookie, right where you want them!

Candy Crazy—Frost cookies with any frosting, then sprinkle with crushed or tiny candy; shake off excess.

Butterflies—Frost cookies with any frosting. Make butterflies by pressing candy-coated chocolate candies into frosting for body and two yogurt-covered mini pretzels into frosting for wings.

Stencil It—Frost cookies with glaze*. When the glaze is completely dry, decorate one cookie at a time by placing a stencil (available at stores that carry baking supplies or online) over the cookie. Sprinkle with edible glitter, then carefully remove the stencil, or tint glaze with food color and drizzle over stencil.

Lollipops—Insert a lollipop stick about 1 inch into the side of each flattened cookie dough ball on the cookie sheet before baking. When cooled, dip the cookies in the glaze* and shake off the excess. Decorate as desired.

Splattered Up—Spoon glaze* into several small bowls; tint with different food colors. Drizzle the cookies with different-colored glazes for a splattered look.

Dip 'n Decorate—Dip half of each cookie into glaze*; place on cooling rack (place a piece of waxed or cooking parchment paper under cooling rack to catch drips). Immediately decorate with sprinkles, mini chocolate chips or coconut; let glaze dry.

Sunny Smiles—Frost cookies with glaze* tinted yellow with food color. While glaze is still wet, press candy corn, pointed ends out, in a circle around edge of cookie to form sun shapes. When glaze is dry, make eyes and smiles inside sun using black decorator's icing.

*Glaze

3 tablespoons butter, melted
1 cup powdered sugar
1 teaspoon regular or clear vanilla
1 to 3 tablespoons milk

In medium bowl, mix butter, powdered sugar and vanilla. Stir in milk, 1 tablespoon at a time, until desired glaze consistency. Makes about ½ cup glaze.

Peanut Butter–Toffee Turtle Cookies

Prep Time: 20 Minutes • **Start to Finish:** 35 Minutes • 3 dozen cookies

½ cup unsalted butter, softened

½ cup granulated sugar

½ cup packed light brown sugar

⅔ cup creamy peanut butter

1 egg

2 cups Original Bisquick® mix

⅔ cup toffee bits

⅔ cup coarsely chopped peanuts

1⅓ cups milk chocolate chips

1½ cups caramels (from 14-oz bag), unwrapped

2 to 3 tablespoons whipping cream

½ teaspoon vanilla

1 Heat oven to 350°F. In large bowl, beat butter, granulated sugar, brown sugar and peanut butter with electric mixer on medium speed until creamy. Beat in egg until blended. Add Bisquick mix, beating on low speed just until blended. Stir in toffee bits, peanuts and ⅔ cup of the chocolate chips.

2 Onto ungreased cookie sheets, drop dough by rounded tablespoonfuls 2 inches apart; flatten with hand.

3 Bake 10 to 12 minutes or until golden brown. Cool 1 minute; remove from cookie sheets to cooling racks.

4 In microwavable bowl, microwave caramels and 2 tablespoons of the whipping cream uncovered on High 1 minute; stir. Microwave 1 minute longer, stirring every 30 seconds, until caramels are melted and mixture is smooth; add remaining 1 tablespoon whipping cream, if necessary. Stir in vanilla. Spoon caramel mixture onto tops of cookies. In small microwavable bowl, microwave remaining ⅔ cup chocolate chips on High 30 to 60 seconds or until melted. Drizzle over caramel.

1 Cookie: Calories 216; Total Fat 12g (Saturated Fat 5g; Trans Fat 0g); Cholesterol 0mg; Sodium 149mg; Total Carbohydrate 26g (Dietary Fiber 1g); Protein 4g **Exchanges:** 2 Other Carbohydrate, ½ High-Fat Meat, 1½ Fat **Carbohydrate Choices:** 2

Gluten-Free Chocolate Crinkles

Prep Time: 1 Hour 20 Minutes • **Start to Finish:** 4 Hours 20 Minutes • **6 dozen cookies**

½ cup vegetable oil

4 oz unsweetened baking chocolate, melted, cooled

2 cups granulated sugar

2 teaspoons gluten-free vanilla

4 eggs

2½ cups Bisquick® Gluten Free mix

½ cup powdered sugar

1 In large bowl, mix oil, chocolate, granulated sugar and vanilla. Stir in eggs, one at a time until blended. Stir in Bisquick mix until dough forms. Cover; refrigerate at least 3 hours.

2 Heat oven to 350°F. Grease cookie sheets with shortening or cooking spray (without flour). Place powdered sugar in small shallow bowl. Drop dough by teaspoonfuls into powdered sugar; roll around to coat and shape into balls. On cookie sheets, place balls about 2 inches apart.

3 Bake 10 to 12 minutes or until almost no imprint remains when touched lightly in center. Immediately remove from cookie sheets to cooling racks.

1 Cookie: Calories 60; Total Fat 2g (Saturated Fat 0g; Trans Fat 0g); Cholesterol 10mg; Sodium 50mg; Total Carbohydrate 10g (Dietary Fiber 0g); Protein 0g **Exchanges:** ½ Other Carbohydrate, ½ Fat **Carbohydrate Choices:** ½

If you are cooking gluten free, always read labels to make sure each recipe ingredient is gluten free. Products and ingredient sources can change.

To save time and cleanup, tear off several sheets of foil to use as cookie sheet liners. Simply bake cookies as directed, greasing the foil as you would the cookie sheet. Or you can use parchment paper and you don't need to grease it at all.

Fudgy Frosted Brownie Cookies

Prep Time: 1 Hour 15 Minutes • **Start to Finish:** 1 Hour 15 Minutes • 1½ **dozen cookies**

COOKIES

- 1 **cup Original Bisquick® mix**
- ¾ **cup granulated sugar**
- ⅔ **cup chopped pecans**
- ½ **cup unsweetened baking cocoa**
- ½ **cup sour cream**
- 1 **teaspoon vanilla**
- 1 **egg**

FROSTING

- 2 **oz unsweetened baking chocolate**
- 2 **tablespoons butter**
- 2 **cups powdered sugar**
- 3 **to 4 tablespoons hot water**

1 Heat oven to 350°F. Spray cookie sheets with cooking spray.

2 In medium bowl, stir all cookie ingredients until well blended.

3 Onto cookie sheets, drop dough by rounded tablespoonfuls about 2 inches apart.

4 Bake 9 to 11 minutes or until set. Cool 2 minutes; remove from cookie sheets to cooling racks. Cool completely, about 30 minutes.

5 In 2-quart saucepan, melt chocolate and butter over low heat, stirring occasionally. Remove from heat. Stir in powdered sugar and 3 tablespoons of the hot water until smooth. (If frosting is too thick, add additional water, 1 teaspoon at a time.) Spread frosting over cookies.

1 Cookie: Calories 200; Total Fat 9g (Saturated Fat 3.5g; Trans Fat 0g); Cholesterol 20mg; Sodium 100mg; Total Carbohydrate 29g (Dietary Fiber 2g); Protein 2g **Exchanges:** ½ Starch, 1½ Other Carbohydrate, 1½ Fat **Carbohydrate Choices:** 2

> Make these fudgy chocolate cookies a holiday favorite by frosting with your favorite vanilla frosting and sprinkling with crushed peppermint candies.

Gluten-Free Snickerdoodles

Prep Time: 50 Minutes • **Start to Finish:** 50 Minutes • 2½ dozen cookies

2 eggs

1¼ cups sugar

¼ cup butter, softened

¼ cup shortening

2 cups Bisquick® Gluten Free mix

2 teaspoons ground cinnamon

1 Heat oven to 375°F. In large bowl, mix eggs, 1 cup of the sugar, the butter and shortening. Stir in Bisquick mix until dough forms.

2 In small bowl, mix remaining ¼ cup sugar and the cinnamon. Shape dough into 30 (1¼-inch) balls. (If dough feels too soft for shaping into balls, place in freezer 10 to 15 minutes.) Roll balls in cinnamon-sugar; place 2 inches apart on ungreased cookie sheets.

3 Bake 10 to 12 minutes or until set. Immediately remove from cookie sheets to cooling racks.

1 Cookie: Calories 100; Total Fat 4g (Saturated Fat 1.5g; Trans Fat 0g); Cholesterol 20mg; Sodium 105mg; Total Carbohydrate 15g (Dietary Fiber 0g); Protein 1g **Exchanges:** ½ Starch, ½ Other Carbohydrate, ½ Fat **Carbohydrate Choices:** 1

If you are cooking gluten free, always read labels to make sure each recipe ingredient is gluten free. Products and ingredient sources can change.

These rich cinnamon-sugar cookies make a great gift! Place a bag of them in a small basket along with packets of cappuccino or hot chocolate mix.

Gluten-Free Chocolate Chip Snickerdoodles

Prep Time: 45 Minutes • **Start to Finish:** 1 Hour • 40 cookies

2 eggs

1¼ cups sugar

¼ cup butter, softened

¼ cup shortening

2 cups Bisquick® Gluten Free mix

½ cup miniature semisweet chocolate chips

1 tablespoon unsweetened baking cocoa

2 teaspoons ground cinnamon

1 Heat oven to 375°F. In large bowl, mix eggs, 1 cup of the sugar, the butter and shortening. Stir in Bisquick mix and chocolate chips until dough forms.

2 In small bowl, mix remaining ¼ cup sugar, the cocoa and cinnamon. Shape dough into 40 (1¼-inch) balls. (If dough feels too soft for shaping, place in freezer 10 to 15 minutes.) Roll balls in sugar mixture. On ungreased cookie sheets, place balls 2 inches apart.

3 Bake 9 to 11 minutes or until set. Immediately remove from cookie sheets to cooling racks. Store cooled cookies tightly covered.

1 Cookie: Calories 80; Total Fat 3.5g (Saturated Fat 1.5g; Trans Fat 0g); Cholesterol 0mg; Sodium 65mg; Total Carbohydrate 13g (Dietary Fiber 0g); Protein 1g **Exchanges:** ½ Other Carbohydrate, ½ Fat **Carbohydrate Choices:** ½

> If you are cooking gluten free, always read labels to make sure each recipe ingredient is gluten free. Products and ingredient sources can change.

Gluten-Free Lemon Squares

Prep Time: 15 Minutes • **Start to Finish:** 4 Hours • **16 squares**

1 cup Bisquick® Gluten Free mix

½ cup butter, softened

¼ cup powdered sugar

1 cup granulated sugar

2 teaspoons grated lemon peel

3 tablespoons fresh lemon juice

½ teaspoon baking powder

¼ teaspoon salt

2 eggs

2 tablespoons butter, melted

Powdered sugar

1 Heat oven to 350°F. In medium bowl, stir Bisquick mix, ½ cup butter and ¼ cup powdered sugar until blended. (Mixture will be crumbly.) Press in bottom of ungreased 8-inch square pan.

2 Bake 18 to 22 minutes or until light golden brown.

3 In medium bowl, mix granulated sugar, lemon peel, lemon juice, baking powder, salt and eggs with electric mixer on medium speed 3 minutes or until light and fluffy. Beat in melted butter. Pour over hot crust.

4 Bake 25 to 26 minutes or until no indentation remains when touched lightly in center. Cool completely in pan on cooling rack, about 1 hour. Refrigerate 2 hours or until well chilled. Sprinkle with powdered sugar. Cut into 4 rows by 4 rows. Store covered in refrigerator.

1 Square: Calories 160; Total Fat 8g (Saturated Fat 5g; Trans Fat 0g); Cholesterol 0mg; Sodium 170mg; Total Carbohydrate 21g (Dietary Fiber 0g); Protein 1g **Exchanges:** ½ Starch, 1 Other Carbohydrate, 1½ Fat **Carbohydrate Choices:** 1½

> If you are cooking gluten free, always read labels to make sure each recipe ingredient is gluten free. Products and ingredient sources can change.

Raspberry Bars

Prep Time: 10 Minutes • **Start to Finish:** 1 Hour 40 Minutes • 24 bars

2 cups Original Bisquick® mix

1 cup quick-cooking oats

¾ cup packed brown sugar

½ cup butter, softened

1 cup raspberry spreadable fruit, jam or preserves

1 Heat oven to 400°F. Spray 9-inch square pan with cooking spray.

2 In large bowl, mix Bisquick mix, oats and brown sugar. Cut in butter, using pastry blender or fork, until mixture looks like coarse crumbs.

3 Press half of crumb mixture in pan. Spread fruit over crumb mixture in pan to within ¼ inch of edges. Top with remaining crumb mixture; press gently into fruit.

4 Bake 25 to 30 minutes or until light brown. Cool completely, about 1 hour. Cut into 6 rows by 4 rows.

1 Bar: Calories 150; Total Fat 5g (Saturated Fat 3g; Trans Fat 0.5g); Cholesterol 10mg; Sodium 160mg; Total Carbohydrate 25g (Dietary Fiber 0g); Protein 1g **Exchanges:** ½ Starch, 1 Other Carbohydrate, 1 Fat **Carbohydrate Choices:** 1½

Substitute blackberry spreadable fruit for the raspberry spreadable fruit.

To soften brown sugar that is hard, place the sugar in a microwavable glass bowl. Cover the bowl with a damp paper towel and then with plastic wrap. Microwave on High 1 minute and let stand covered for 2 minutes. If it is still hard, repeat microwaving for 1 minute.

Gluten-Free Toffee–Peanut Butter Bars

Prep Time: 10 Minutes • **Start to Finish:** 1 Hour 35 Minutes • 24 bars

2 tablespoons sugar

1 can (14 oz) sweetened condensed milk (not evaporated)

1 cup gluten-free peanut butter

2 cups Bisquick® Gluten Free mix

1 teaspoon gluten-free vanilla

1 cup toffee bits

3 bars (3.52 oz each) Swiss milk chocolate with honey and almond nougat, finely chopped

1 Heat oven to 350°F. Grease 13x9-inch pan with shortening. Sprinkle bottom of pan with sugar; tap out excess.

2 In large bowl, beat condensed milk and peanut butter with electric mixer on medium speed until creamy. Add Bisquick mix and vanilla; beat on low speed until blended. Stir in ½ cup of the toffee bits. Press in pan.

3 Bake 16 to 18 minutes or until very light brown (crust will be soft). Immediately sprinkle chopped chocolate evenly over hot bars. Let stand 5 minutes to soften; gently spread chocolate with spatula. Sprinkle with remaining ½ cup toffee bits. Refrigerate until set, about 1 hour. Cut into 6 rows by 4 rows. Store tightly covered at room temperature.

1 Bar: Calories 280; Total Fat 13g (Saturated Fat 5g; Trans Fat 0g); Cholesterol 0mg; Sodium 210mg; Total Carbohydrate 35g (Dietary Fiber 0g); Protein 5g **Exchanges:** ½ Starch, 1½ Other Carbohydrate, ½ High-Fat Meat, 1½ Fat **Carbohydrate Choices:** 2

> If you are cooking gluten free, always read labels to make sure each recipe ingredient is gluten free. Products and ingredient sources can change.

Mississippi Mud Bars

Prep Time: 20 Minutes • **Start to Finish:** 4 Hours 5 Minutes • **36 bars**

⅓ cup butter

5 oz unsweetened baking chocolate

¾ cup Original Bisquick® mix

¾ cup plus 2 tablespoons granulated sugar

2 teaspoons vanilla

2 eggs

1½ cups miniature marshmallows

1 tablespoon butter

⅔ cup sour cream

1⅓ cups powdered sugar

1 Heat oven to 350°F. Grease and flour 9-inch square pan. In 1½-quart saucepan, melt ⅓ cup butter and 2½ oz of the chocolate over low heat, stirring frequently. Cool slightly, about 15 minutes.

2 In medium bowl, beat chocolate mixture, Bisquick mix, granulated sugar, vanilla and eggs with electric mixer on low speed 30 seconds, scraping bowl frequently. Beat on medium speed 1 minute. Spread batter in pan.

3 Bake 20 to 25 minutes or until toothpick inserted in center comes out clean. Remove from oven; immediately sprinkle with marshmallows. Cover; let stand about 5 minutes or until marshmallows soften. Uncover; cool completely, about 1 hour.

4 In 1½-quart saucepan, melt remaining 2½ oz chocolate and 1 tablespoon butter; cool slightly. Stir in sour cream and powdered sugar until smooth. Spread over marshmallow layer. Cover; refrigerate at least 2 hours or until firm. Cut into 6 rows by 6 rows. Store in refrigerator.

1 Bar: Calories 110; Total Fat 6g (Saturated Fat 3.5g, Trans Fat 0g); Cholesterol 20mg; Sodium 55mg; Total Carbohydrate 14g (Dietary Fiber 0g); Protein 1g **Exchanges:** 1 Other Carbohydrate, 1 Fat **Carbohydrate Choices:** 1

Rocky Road Bars

Prep Time: 15 Minutes • **Start to Finish:** 45 Minutes • 30 bars

1 cup semisweet chocolate chips

2 tablespoons butter

2 cups Original Bisquick® mix

1 cup sugar

½ teaspoon vanilla

2 eggs

1 cup miniature marshmallows

¼ cup chopped nuts, if desired

1 Heat oven to 350°F. Grease bottom only of 13x9-inch pan. In 1-quart saucepan, heat ½ cup of the chocolate chips and the butter over low heat, stirring occasionally, until melted.

2 Mix Bisquick mix, sugar, vanilla and eggs into chocolate mixture; spread in pan. Bake 15 minutes.

3 Sprinkle with marshmallows, nuts and remaining ½ cup chocolate chips. Bake 10 to 15 minutes longer or until marshmallows are light brown. Cool completely. Cut into 6 rows by 5 rows.

1 Bar: Calories 115; Total Fat 5g (Saturated Fat 2g, Trans Fat 0g); Cholesterol 15mg; Sodium 130mg; Total Carbohydrate 17g (Dietary Fiber 0g); Protein 1g **Exchanges:** 1 Starch, 1 Fat **Carbohydrate Choices:** 1

Pumpkin-Caramel Cheesecake Bars

Prep Time: 10 Minutes • **Start to Finish:** 3 Hours 10 Minutes • 24 bars

1⅓ cups Bisquick Heart Smart® mix

½ cup packed brown sugar

¼ cup chopped pecans, toasted*

¼ cup cold butter

2 packages (8 oz each) ⅓-less-fat cream cheese (Neufchâtel), softened

2 tablespoons Bisquick Heart Smart® mix

1½ cups packed brown sugar

1 container (6 oz) vanilla thick and creamy low-fat yogurt

1 can (15 oz) pumpkin (not pumpkin pie mix)

¾ cup fat-free egg product

¼ cup caramel fat-free topping

Additional chopped pecans, if desired

Additional caramel topping, if desired

1 Heat oven to 375°F. In medium bowl, mix 1⅓ cups Bisquick mix, ½ cup brown sugar and the toasted pecans. Cut in butter, using pastry blender or fork, until mixture looks like coarse crumbs. Pat into bottom of ungreased 15x10x1-inch pan.

2 Bake 10 minutes.

3 In large bowl, beat cream cheese, 2 tablespoons Bisquick mix and 1½ cups brown sugar on medium speed until fluffy. Beat in yogurt, pumpkin, egg product and ¼ cup caramel topping on low speed until blended. Pour over partially baked crust.

4 Bake 45 to 50 minutes or until knife inserted in center comes out clean.

5 Cool completely on cooling rack, about 2 hours. Garnish with additional pecans and caramel topping. Cut into 6 rows by 4 rows. Store covered in refrigerator.

*To toast pecans, cook in an ungreased skillet over medium heat 5 to 7 minutes, stirring frequently, until golden brown.

1 Bar: Calories 190; Total Fat 7g (Saturated Fat 3.5g; Trans Fat 0g); Cholesterol 15mg; Sodium 190mg; Total Carbohydrate 29g (Dietary Fiber 0g); Protein 4g **Exchanges:** 1 Starch, 1 Other Carbohydrate, 1½ Fat **Carbohydrate Choices:** 2

Make sure the cream cheese is softened so that it quickly blends in with the other ingredients. Beat the batter just until smooth; overbeating can cause a dry cheesecake.

Serve with a dollop of caramel-flavored whipped cream. In a chilled small bowl, beat ½ cup whipping cream and 1 tablespoon caramel fat-free topping on high speed until soft peaks form.

Metric Conversion Guide

VOLUME

U.S. Units	Canadian Metric	Australian Metric
¼ teaspoon	1 mL	1 ml
½ teaspoon	2 mL	2 ml
1 teaspoon	5 mL	5 ml
1 tablespoon	15 mL	20 ml
¼ cup	50 mL	60 ml
⅓ cup	75 mL	80 ml
½ cup	125 mL	125 ml
⅔ cup	150 mL	170 ml
¾ cup	175 mL	190 ml
1 cup	250 mL	250 ml
1 quart	1 liter	1 liter
1½ quarts	1.5 liters	1.5 liters
2 quarts	2 liters	2 liters
2½ quarts	2.5 liters	2.5 liters
3 quarts	3 liters	3 liters
4 quarts	4 liters	4 liters

WEIGHT

U.S. Units	Canadian Metric	Australian Metric
1 ounce	30 grams	30 grams
2 ounces	55 grams	60 grams
3 ounces	85 grams	90 grams
4 ounces (¼ pound)	115 grams	125 grams
8 ounces (½ pound)	225 grams	225 grams
16 ounces (1 pound)	455 grams	500 grams
1 pound	455 grams	500 grams

MEASUREMENTS

Inches	Centimeters
1	2.5
2	5.0
3	7.5
4	10.0
5	12.5
6	15.0
7	17.5
8	20.5
9	23.0
10	25.5
11	28.0
12	30.5
13	33.0

TEMPERATURES

Fahrenheit	Celsius
32°	0°
212°	100°
250°	120°
275°	140°
300°	150°
325°	160°
350°	180°
375°	190°
400°	200°
425°	220°
450°	230°
475°	240°
500°	260°

Note: The recipes in this cookbook have not been developed or tested using metric measures. When converting recipes to metric, some variations in quality may be noted.

index

Page numbers in *italic* indicate illustrations. * indicates calorie-controlled recipes. # indicates quick recipes.

Recipe Testing and Calculating Nutrition Information

Recipe Testing:

- Large eggs and 2% milk were used unless otherwise indicated.

- Fat-free, low-fat, low-sodium or lite products were not used unless indicated.

- No nonstick cookware and bakeware were used unless otherwise indicated. No dark-colored, black or insulated bakeware was used.

- When a pan is specified, a metal pan was used; a baking dish or pie plate means ovenproof glass was used.

- An electric hand mixer was used for mixing only when mixer speeds are specified.

Calculating Nutrition:

- The first ingredient was used wherever a choice is given, such as ⅓ cup sour cream or plain yogurt.

- The first amount was used wherever a range is given, such as 3- to 3½-pound whole chicken.

- The first serving number was used wherever a range is given, such as 4 to 6 servings.

- "If desired" ingredients were not included.

- Only the amount of a marinade or frying oil that is absorbed was included.